THE
OBAMA
EDUCATION PLAN

EDUCATION WEEK

Education Week is the nation's premier independent news source for K–12 education. Commonly referred to as "American Education's Newspaper of Record," the nonprofit newspaper has kept educators and policymakers abreast of important developments in schools for more than 27 years. *Education Week* boasts a staff of more than 30 reporters and editors, each and every one an expert in the complicated world of covering education. Increasingly, *Education Week* is focusing on coverage that seeks to help policymakers and practitioners identify "what works," promising strategies, and model programs.

Education Week Press is one arm of Editorial Projects in Education (EPE), an independent, nonprofit corporation dedicated to elevating the level of discourse on American K–12 education and best known as the publisher of *Education Week*. EPE is also the home of teachermagazine.org, TopSchoolJobs.org, Digital Directions, and the EPE Research Center, which produces the highly acclaimed *Quality Counts, Technology Counts,* and *Diplomas Counts* reports. EPE's Web site, edweek.org, is an award-winning source of up-to-the-minute news, information, and resources for educators, as well as in-depth research on issues preK–12.

THE
OBAMA
EDUCATION PLAN

AN *EDUCATION WEEK* GUIDE

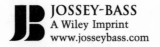

JOSSEY-BASS
A Wiley Imprint
www.josseybass.com

14.95

Library of Congress Cataloging-in-Publication Data has been applied for.

ISBN 978-047-048209-4

Printed in the United States of America

FIRST EDITION

PB Printing   10~9~8~7~6~5~4~3~2

Contents

Introduction
A Mandate for Change

DURING A PRESIDENTIAL CAMPAIGN in which the candidates held few substantive debates about educational issues, Senator Barack Obama's campaign proposals stood out for their breadth, detail, and ambitious goals.

"Michelle and I are only here tonight because we were given a chance at an education. And I will not settle for an America where some kids don't have that chance," he said while accepting the Democratic nomination on August 28. "I'll invest in early childhood education. I'll recruit an army of new teachers, and pay them higher salaries, and give them more support. And in exchange, I'll ask for higher standards and more accountability."

The plans don't stop there. Mr. Obama proposed a tuition tax credit to college students who promise to teach in hard-to-staff schools or complete 100 hours of community service. He said he would change the No Child Left Behind Act to encourage states to use tests that measure students' higher-order thinking skills. He wants the law to emphasize honoring good schools instead of identifying underperforming ones. He also said he would double the amount spent on educational research and development. In total, the proposals would add $18 billion in federal K–12 spending and another $12 billion for higher education costs.

Leaders of the education policy community are eager to hear when and how Mr. Obama's administration will address the wide-ranging issues he outlined during the campaign. Which issues will be tackled first? What compromises will need to be made? And how will the economic recession and financial credit crisis affect the pace and scope of change? This book offers both news articles and opinion from the archives of *Education Week* to help inform the debates over these issues as the Obama administration's education policies take shape.

ABOUT THIS BOOK

Part One of this book is organized around the main points of the Obama-Biden Education Plan—from investment in early childhood education to improving college affordability. Each chapter begins with a brief summary of the issue (drawn or synthesized from information on Obama's campaign site) and lists Obama's major proposals for change as stated by his campaign. This is followed by a "Perspectives" section, which is composed of material from the *Education Week* archives—relevant articles, stories about innovative programs, and provocative opinion pieces (called "Commentary"). The Obama-Biden proposals covered a lot of ground—so, for simplicity's sake, we combined some items. For example, the three parts of the early childhood education plan are addressed in Chapter 1, and college outreach/accessibility articles are combined with college finance articles in Chapter 8. Finally, the proposals to address the Dropout Crisis, expand high-quality after-school opportunities, and support English-language learners are divided between Chapters 5 and 6.

Part Two contains excerpts from two presidential advice projects. Chapter 9 is drawn from the "Education Advice for President-elect Obama," a multimedia project produced by Learning Matters. Learning Matters collected advice for the president from teachers, administrators, policymakers, and students, and distributed it via podcasts, broadcasts, and postings on its website EdAdviceFor Obama.org. Due to space constraints, we could only include a fraction of the advice from people with diverse roles and perspectives in education. Chapter 10 summarizes key policy recommendations for the new administration from the National Academy of Education.

The Obama campaign was noteworthy for its outreach and engagement with the public. Therefore, it's no surprise that Barack Obama's education plan—along with documents detailing proposals for Pre-K–12, Education Reform, and College Affordability—has long been available on the website barackobama.com. During the transition, the plan could also be viewed at the change.gov site. For reference, we've included this version of the Obama-Biden education plan at the end of this book.

HOPE FOR THE FUTURE

President Obama's goals for education will take an extraordinary level of leadership, resources, consensus, and collaborative will to enact. We hope this book will serve as a useful road map to the hard work ahead. In addition, we hope it will provide valuable insights on the complex issues at hand as the Obama-Biden proposals are debated, legislated, and implemented in the years to come.

Acknowledgments

THE ARTICLES printed in this book reflect the work of numerous *Education Week* reporters. In addition, Mary-Ellen Phelps Deily of Education Week Press compiled articles for this book. David J. Hoff of *Education Week* contributed to this book's introduction. The editors at Jossey-Bass developed or adapted the chapter-opening "The Issue" and "The Obama Plan" sections working with information available on the websites barackobama.com and change.gov.

Education Week would like to acknowledge the support of the following foundations for reporting of articles included in this book. As a nonprofit organization, Editorial Projects in Education—*Education Week*'s nonprofit parent company—receives underwriting from these organizations and others:

Coverage of new schooling arrangements and classroom improvement efforts is supported by a grant from the Annenberg Foundation.

Coverage of public education in New Orleans is underwritten by a grant from the Ford Foundation.

Coverage of mathematics, science, and technology education is supported by a grant from the Ewing Marion Kauffman Foundation.

Special coverage marking the 25th anniversary of the landmark report "A Nation at Risk" is supported in part by a grant from the Eli and Edythe Broad Foundation.

Coverage of education research is supported in part by a grant from the Spencer Foundation.

Coverage of policy efforts to improve the teaching profession is supported by a grant from the Joyce Foundation.

Coverage of pathways to college and careers is underwritten in part by a grant from the Carnegie Corporation of New York.

Coverage of graduation rates and reporting and research for the EPE Research Center's annual *Diplomas Count* report is underwritten by the Bill & Melinda Gates Foundation.

Finally, thanks to Anique Halliday, Selly Thiam, Elena Schilder, and Donald Devet of Learning Matters for allowing us to transcribe and print audio selections from their "Advice to the President-Elect" project. Also thanks to Greg White, executive director of the National Academy of Education, for permission to use the NAEd white paper recommendations.

PART ONE

THE EDUCATION PLAN

"This agenda starts with education. Whether you're conservative or liberal, Republican or Democrat, practically every economist agrees that in this digital age, a highly educated and skilled workforce will be the key not only to individual opportunity, but to the overall success of our economy as well. We cannot be satisfied until every child in America—and I mean every child—has the same chances for a good education that we want for our own children."

BARACK OBAMA
Flint, Mich., June 16, 2008

CHAPTER I

Invest in Early Childhood Education

"We know what a difference early childhood programs
make in the lives of our kids."

BARACK OBAMA

Manchester, N.H., November 20, 2007

THE ISSUE

*The time has come to put children first by focusing investments
where research and effective practice tell us we will have the
greatest opportunity for long-term success.*

*Research shows that early experiences shape whether
a child's brain develops strong skills for future learning,
behavior, and success. Investing in early learning also makes
economic sense. For every dollar invested in high-quality,
comprehensive programs supporting children and families
from birth, there is a $7–$10 return to society in decreased
need for special education services, higher graduation and
employment rates, less crime, less use of the public welfare
system, and better health.*

*The infant and toddler years are particularly critical,
because many children spend significant parts of their day
with caretakers other than their parents. In addition to
ensuring that child care is accessible and affordable, we
must do more to ensure that it is high quality and provides
the educational experiences our children need.*

THE OBAMA PLAN

Investment in children is not just morally right— these investments raise productivity of society as a whole. The Obama-Biden plan includes proposals for:

- **Zero to Five Plan**: The comprehensive "Zero to Five" plan will provide critical support to young children and their parents. It places key emphasis at early care and education for infants, which is essential for children to be ready to enter kindergarten. Obama and Biden will create Early Learning Challenge Grants to promote state Zero to Five efforts and help states move toward voluntary, universal preschool.

- **Expand Early Head Start and Head Start**: Quadruple Early Head Start, increase Head Start funding, and improve quality for both.

- **Provide Affordable, High-Quality Child Care**: Increase access to affordable and high-quality child care to ease the burden on working families.

PERSPECTIVES

．　．　．

LONG-TERM PAYOFF SEEN FROM EARLY-CHILDHOOD EDUCATION

BY LINDA JACOBSON
June 11, 2008

THE LATEST ANALYSIS of a long-running early-childhood-education program for children of low-income families in Chicago suggests economic payoffs from such services that continue well into adulthood.

Researchers looking at data from the study, which is now more than 20 years old, say that for every dollar spent on children who attended the Chicago Child Parent Centers, almost $10 is returned by age 25 in either benefits to society—such as savings on remediation in school and on the criminal-justice system—or to the participant, in the form of higher earnings.

"The study is significant, given it is the only one of a sustained public school program and one of the very few which go into adulthood," Arthur J. Reynolds, a child-development professor at the

University of Minnesota-Twin Cities and the lead researcher on the project, said in an e-mail.

He added that the benefits are probably underestimated because he has found some unexpected outcomes, such as participants' being more likely than those in the comparison group to hold private health insurance and less likely to have mental-health problems.

But some experts caution that the children served by the Chicago program and similar efforts were very disadvantaged, and that providing such services to middle-class families in universal preschool programs are unlikely to result in the same return on investment.

"The biggest argument against the Chicago economic data is that it is still largely a 'boutique' program that cost more and provided more services than most current universal and preschool programs," said Lisa Snell, the director of education and child welfare at the Los Angeles-based Reason Foundation, a free-market-oriented think tank. "It is hard to imagine that current programs will have the same kinds of economic payoffs as the Chicago program."

The State of Preschool

More than one million 3- and 4-year-olds now attend public preschool programs in the United States, but 12 states still don't have publicly financed programs, according to the newest yearbook from the National Institute for Early Education Research at Rutgers University in New Brunswick, N.J.

Released annually since 2004, the report tracks state developments in offering early-childhood-education programs. It ranks states on the percentage of eligible children enrolled and on 10 measures of quality, such as having teachers with bachelor's degrees, providing comprehensive services in addition to education activities, and providing nutritious meals.

The report also takes a particularly close look at four states—California, Florida, Ohio, and Texas—which enroll the bulk of children served in those programs, but meet fewer than half the 10 quality benchmarks.

The conclusions were presented late last month at a meeting in San Francisco of the Society for Prevention Research, based in Fairfax, Va.

Parent Involvement

The Chicago Longitudinal Study originally included 1,539 children from low-income African-American and Hispanic families who began in the early-education program run by the Chicago school system at 25 sites in either 1985 or 1986.

The Chicago program began in 1967 at sites in or near elementary schools. Similar to the federal Head Start program, the Child-Parent Centers provide comprehensive education, health, and family-support services to children ages 3 to 9.

Unlike in Head Start, all the teachers in the program have bachelor's degrees and are paid at the same level as K–12 teachers.

In addition, parents are expected to participate in the classroom—a component that distinguishes the Chicago program from

---

"The nation made progress this year, but when you dig deep into the data, the picture is not so rosy," W. Steven Barnett, the director of the institute, said in a statement.

Among the children who still don't attend government-financed preschool, he added, most are from middle-class families that cannot afford expensive private preschools.

"States must decide whether education of young children will continue to be a welfare program for the poor or an essential investment in all Americans," Mr. Barnett said.

Other key findings include the first increase in overall per-pupil spending since the report was initially released. The average amount spent per child, $3,642, however, is still $700 less than the level spent in 2001–02 when adjusted for inflation, the report says. The spending trends, according to the report, suggest "that states are struggling to maintain spending levels in light of enrollment increases and inflation."

By Linda Jacobson   March 26, 2008

other early-intervention initiatives—and the children in the study received home visits from a "school-community representative."

"The parents were expected to get involved, and there were 30 different ways [for parents to participate], so nobody said no," Mr. Reynolds said.

While the study was not designed as a true randomized trial, a comparison group including children who were matched to the participants on socioeconomic factors and demographic variables, such as family size and parents' employment status, has been used to track the effectiveness of the intervention. Children in the comparison group took part in other early-childhood programs, such as Head Start, or full-day kindergarten.

Last year, Mr. Reynolds released findings in the *Archives of Pediatrics and Adolescent Medicine*, a monthly journal, based on study of participants at age 24. Those findings showed that the adults had acquired more education and were less likely to commit crimes than those who had not received the same level of service.

A Body of Evidence

Because of its evidence of lasting positive effects, such as lower special education costs and less welfare dependency, Mr. Reynolds' study on the Chicago program is often used as one of three long-running research projects to argue for public spending on early-childhood education. The other two are the High/Scope Perry Preschool study, which ran in Ypsilanti, Mich., outside Detroit from 1962 to 1967, and the Carolina Abecedarian Project, in Chapel Hill, N.C., which provided services from birth through age 5 to 112 children from low-income families born between 1972 and 1977.

The Chicago study stands out, however, because it is not a demonstration program as are the others. It has been operated by a public school system and thus is likely more "generalizable to other similar and contemporary locations and contexts," Albert Wat, a state-policy analyst at the Washington-based advocacy group Pre-K Now, wrote last year in the report "Dollars and Sense: A Review of Economic Analyses of Pre-K."

The Chicago program "demonstrates that public schools can effectively implement high-quality pre-K programs that produce long-term positive gains," he wrote.

Still, Mr. Reynolds concludes that the newest "evidence strengthens the findings of a high return on investment of public programs, if they follow the key principles of effectiveness."

Mr. Reynolds' new analysis, which will be released in a research paper later this year, also provides a comparison of the economic benefits of various types of preschool programs.

It uses an average of all the cost-benefit studies that have been conducted on other popular policies, such as full-day kindergarten, class-size reduction, and the federal Women, Infants, and Children, or wic, nutrition program.

The comparison shows that preschool programs have by far the highest return, $6.02 for every $1 spent, compared with $2.47 for small classes, $3.07 for wic, and nothing for full-day kindergarten.

· · ·

FINE-TUNING PRESCHOOL RATING SYSTEMS

BY LINDA JACOBSON
October 29, 2008

THE USE OF RATING SCALES as a way to encourage child-care centers and preschools to improve their programs continues to increase in popularity across the states, even as researchers say states need to do more to share what they find and to demonstrate whether rating systems improve children's learning.

Last month, California Gov. Arnold Schwarzenegger, a Republican, signed a bill creating an advisory committee that will begin the process of designing a scale for the state, which has lagged behind others on indicators of preschool classroom quality.

In Washington state, the department of early learning is set to begin piloting its new Seeds of Success quality rating and improvement system with 125 providers in five communities.

And in Virginia, Gov. Tim Kaine's new office of early childhood development is in the second year of field testing its new Star Quality system with 350 state-funded pre-K, Head Start, and private child-care classrooms.

But a recent study by researchers at the Santa Monica, Calif.-based RAND Corp. suggests that officials haven't done a great job of sharing what they've learned from operating these programs.

Gail L. Zellman and Michal Perlman gathered representatives from five states that were among the first to implement what are known as quality rating and improvement systems: Colorado, North Carolina, Ohio, Oklahoma, and Pennsylvania.

The researchers wrote that despite the widespread appeal and growth of such systems, "there is a dearth of practical knowledge

Preschool Effects

Preschool can benefit children's learning and development, but the quality of existing preschool initiatives across the country varies tremendously, says a report from the Education and the Public Interest Center at the University of Colorado at Boulder and the Education Policy Research Unit at Arizona State University in Tempe.

High-quality preschool programs can raise achievement scores, reduce grade retention, and reduce the likelihood that students will be referred to special education, author W. Steven Barnett, the director of the National Institute for Early Education Research at Rutgers University in New Brunswick, N.J., writes in the September 10 policy brief.

But because of the uneven quality of programs, he recommends that policymakers avoid handing out more child-care subsidies for preschool and instead focus on expanding effective preschools with high standards.

By Linda Jacobson   September 17, 2008

and empirical data to draw on in crafting qris legislation, design-ing qris and implementing qris components."

They found that the five states included the education and train-ing levels of a center's teachers and measured classroom quality in some way. But states differed on other components of their rating systems, such as whether to include a measure of parent involve-ment or whether a center is nationally accredited.

Several recommendations emerged from the interviews, such as securing funding for programs before the process begins, conducting public-awareness campaigns, and having the experts who rate a cen-ter be different from the ones who provide technical assistance.

Market-Driven Approach

Like health department grades for eating establishments, rating scales are viewed as a market-driven way to encourage centers to increase the level of quality they provide and to better inform par-ents about the centers they are choosing for their children.

The National Child Care Information and Technical Assistance Center, part of the federal government's Child Care Bureau, says 16 states had statewide rating systems as of January, and more than 25 states were exploring or designing them.

In most states, participation is voluntary, but in North Carolina and Tennessee, quality ratings are integrated into the state child-care licensing system. Ratings typically focus on elements such as the teachers' level of education, staff-to-child ratios, and measures of classroom quality.

Most states also attach a continuous-improvement process, which can include funding to improve facilities, purchase learning materials, or work with master teachers. Providers with higher rat-ings can also receive more than the base amount of money from the state for children who are eligible for child-care subsidies.

Outcomes Studied

Evaluations in individual states have shown that rating scales can improve early-childhood-education environments for children.

A 2006 study of Pennsylvania's Keystone STARS Quality Rating System showed that on average, centers participating in the program score higher on measures of quality than those not participating. The researchers, from the University of Pittsburgh Office of Child Development and the Pennsylvania State University Prevention Research Center in University Park, credited the program with reversing a decline in child-care quality in the late 1990s.

But it will take more research to determine if such rating systems contribute to improving children's school-readiness skills.

A separate study that Ms. Zellman and Ms. Perlman conducted on Colorado's Qualistar Early Learning, a nonprofit organization that rates centers, found almost no relationship between the quality rating system and child outcomes such as school readiness, cognitive skills, and social skills.

"While it makes sense and holds general appeal that improved quality will translate into improved child outcomes, the many factors that shape children over time may swamp the association, at least in the short term," they wrote in the study, released earlier this year.

In their interviews, Ms. Zellman and Ms. Perlman found that because many states did not pilot their rating scales before rolling them out across the state, substantial revisions needed to be made.

"What we're hoping to learn from this process is that the system is viable," said Juliet Torres, an assistant director of the Department of Early Learning in Washington state. "We're also looking to see how parents view this information that they receive."

Sandra Giarde, the executive director of the California Association for the Education of Young Children, said her group "is looking forward to having an opportunity to be a participant in the process."

.   .   .

TEACHER-PUPIL LINK CRUCIAL TO PRE-K SUCCESS

BY LINDA JACOBSON

May 21, 2008

THE QUALITY OF THE RELATIONSHIP between preschool teachers and their pupils might be more important to children's learning than such factors as class size and teacher credentials, a new study suggests. That finding could raise questions about traditional measures of preschool quality favored by early-childhood experts and state policymakers.

Using a sample of more than 2,400 4-year-olds in 671 pre-K classrooms in 11 states, researchers at the University of Virginia found that minimum standards for classrooms—including teachers' field of study, their level of education, and the teacher-to-child ratio—were not associated with children's academic, language, and social development.

Instead, academic and language skills were stronger when children received greater instructional support, such as feedback on their ideas and encouragement to think in more complex ways. And children's social skills were more advanced when teachers showed more positive emotions and were sensitive to children's needs.

The study focused on 10 preschool benchmarks measured in an annual report by the National Institute for Early Education Research, a research organization based at Rutgers University in New Brunswick, N.J., that tracks states' efforts to meet preschool-quality indicators.

Those benchmarks include whether states require lead teachers in state-financed preschool programs to have a bachelor's degree, provide at least one meal a day to students, and mandate ongoing training for teachers.

Elements of Quality

"If one were to rest the whole system on those structural indicators that people tend to talk about, you could vastly overestimate the level of quality that is in the system," said Robert C. Pianta, the dean of education at the University of Virginia, in Charlottesville, and one of the authors of the study. It was released last week in the May/June issue of the journal *Child Development*.

Mr. Pianta stressed, however, that the study does not imply that those "elements of program infrastructure" are not important. Instead, both such elements and the supportive qualities identified are needed, he said.

W. Steven Barnett, the director of NIEER, which partially financed the research, said that the study "provides no basis for concluding that the program characteristics associated with the benchmarks are not important for creating programs that are highly effective for all children and meet the broad needs of all of the children they serve."

To conduct the study, the researchers tested children's skills at the beginning and the end of a certain time frame in the program, typically over the course of a school year.

They collected information about whether programs met nine minimum standards of quality recommended by professional organizations, such as the National Association for the Education of Young Children, in Washington.

They also rated the quality of the classroom environment and the interactions between teachers and children, using an instrument devised by Mr. Pianta called CLASS, which stands for Classroom Assessment Scoring System. That assessment tool measures 10 aspects of teaching, divided into three broad categories: instructional support, emotional climate, and classroom organization.

The CLASS instrument has been used as part of the long-running, federally funded Study of Early Child Care and Youth Development. In a 2005 study, Mr. Pianta showed that teachers who give both instructional and emotional support can raise achievement among 1st graders who are considered at risk for school failure because of such factors as poverty and low maternal education levels.

Similar findings were shown for children displaying behavioral and social difficulties: When teachers were warm, sensitive, and positive, the children performed at levels almost identical to those of children without a history of behavior problems.

Mr. Pianta's research also has shown that even within schools or preschool centers, classroom quality varies tremendously, however. Similarly, Mr. Pianta said, even if states or local programs meet minimum benchmarks, the actual environment can be inconsistent across classrooms.

"Once you have those things in place, you still have a long way to go," he said.

CLASS is also being used across the country to train preschool teachers with varying levels of education on how to be more effective in the classroom.

Caution Raised

Mr. Barnett, of NIEER, said its 10 benchmarks are only meant to "set minimums or floors on what programs must do and the human resources they have to do it with."

"None of these [benchmarks] are expected to have direct effects on a child's learning and development," he said.

The requirement for certain health screenings, for example, is intended for children who would not otherwise have the chance to see a doctor.

"Although it is very important for those few children, no one would expect to find an effect on test scores in a study like this one," Mr. Barnett said.

He added that some of the NIEER benchmarks were described differently in the University of Virginia study from the way NIEER explains them, and that two that could have the most influence on teaching practices—state monitoring and professional development—were left out.

Mr. Pianta agreed that state monitoring and professional development are important, but said that they are also "the toughest to get right." Simply requiring a certain number of hours of in-service training might not be very helpful if the training is not focused on interactions with students, he said.

Changes in State Policy

In recent years, state policymakers have responded to the message from preschool experts that high-quality programs are necessary to see lasting benefits for children throughout their school years and beyond.

The 2007 NIEER State Preschool Yearbook noted recent efforts by states to meet more of those benchmarks. The number of states meeting fewer than five indicators fell to eight last year, from nineteen in 2003, and among those eight, Arizona, Kansas, and Maine have changes in the works.

North Carolina's More at Four program and Alabama's preschool program met all ten of the benchmarks. Another eight states have state-funded programs that meet nine of the ten.

But Mr. Pianta added that the use of classroom observation and attention to "what teachers do with kids" is also increasing.

In a press release, Andrew J. Mashburn, the lead author of the study and a senior research scientist at the University of Virginia's Center for Advanced Study of Teaching and Learning, said the results "provide compelling evidence that young children's learning in pre-K occurs in large part through high-quality emotional and instructional interactions with teachers."

Researchers from the University of California, Los Angeles, and the University of North Carolina at Chapel Hill also worked on the study.

. . .

★ ## UNIVERSAL PRE-K: WHAT ABOUT THE BABIES? ★

COMMENTARY BY SAMUEL J. MEISELS
January 25, 2006

TWENTY-FIVE YEARS AGO, I picked up a new book by Jerome Bruner, one of the 20th century's leading developmental psychologists. In the first volume of the Oxford Preschool Project, he wrote something that has stayed with me ever since. He said, "Where emotional and mental growth are concerned, well begun is indeed half done."

Those words have real resonance for me, as an early-childhood educator. I am drawn to their clear recognition that fulfillment in human development is linked to the quality of one's early experiences. But I also see another meaning in Bruner's Aristotelian observation about beginnings and endings. Good beginnings are not enough. Good beginnings, like good intentions, only count when they are sustained, reinforced, and carried through to completion.

The persuasive arguments we've heard about the importance of the early years, from national organizations such as Zero to Three and others, have inspired several generations to improve the care and education of the very young, particularly those at risk. And that work, well begun, has led to dramatic growth in public support for educational and intervention programs prior to kindergarten.

Previously, the largest public investment in pre-K programs was Head Start, which opened as an eight-week summer program in 1965 and today serves more than 900,000 children, many year-round, at a cost in excess of $7 billion. Over the past decade, state-funded pre-K programs have almost surpassed Head Start in the number of children they serve. Pre-K programs are now offered by more than 40 states and the District of Columbia. According to the National Institute for Early Education Research, more than 10 states either have or are considering the option of providing universal pre-K services, though only Georgia and Oklahoma are presently serving all of the 4-year-olds in their states.

This is good news, and everyone who worked to encourage widespread availability of quality pre-K programs for 4-year-olds deserves our thanks and praise. But what about children younger than 4 years of age? If we know that even in infancy—if not in utero—children are establishing critical pathways to later learning and development, what about the babies? One of the most startling statistics about pre-K programs is that 25 states devote no funding whatsoever to those younger than age 4. Their funds are committed solely to the year prior to kindergarten.

Given what we know, is it wise policy to focus on providing care for just 20 percent of the preschool population? Do the pre-K advocates who are working so hard on behalf of the nation's 4-year-olds not care about babies?

Of course they do. The issue is not whether babies are lovable and engaging, or even whether the first years of life are extremely important. Indeed, some advocates within the pre-K movement explain their focus on 4-year-olds by pointing out that their efforts on behalf of pre-K will provide a lever for eventually expanding services to younger children. Nearly all those who are professionally associated with the pre-K movement are also advocates for 3-year-olds and for those between birth and age 3. As one of the leading exponents of prekindergarten wrote to me last summer, "I don't know anyone in the pre-K movement who would not acknowledge the importance of the first three years of life." She went on to note that we must take care not to pit one age group against another, an admonition I take to heart.

But if we allow public policy to turn age 4 into the magical year on which later school success is built, what will we do if nationwide universal pre-K for 4-year-olds fails to deliver on its ambitious promise?

The choice before us is not between supporting pre-K for 4-year-olds or supporting comprehensive services for all children from birth to age 5. I believe that the real task is to clarify—for policymakers and for the public they answer to—the place that the first three or four years of life hold. We know from a National Academy of Sciences report, "From Neurons to Neighborhoods," that the early years matter not because they establish an irreversible pattern of development, but because they furnish us with either a secure or a vulnerable stage on which subsequent development is built. Human development isn't over at age 3. But all the same, it makes sense to start early.

The early years matter not because they establish an irreversible pattern of development, but because they furnish us with either a secure or a vulnerable stage on which subsequent development is built.

The National Scientific Council on the Developing Child points out that the "window of opportunity for development remains open for many years, but the costs of remediation grow with increasing age." Research shows us that starting early has more impact than starting late. As brain circuits are built up and stabilize over time, they become increasingly more difficult to alter. Early intervention makes sense economically and has greater potential for closing the persistent and pernicious achievement gaps that pre-K policy is largely about.

James J. Heckman, the Nobel Prize-winning economist from the University of Chicago, made this point not long ago. He said, "Learning starts in infancy, long before formal education begins, and continues throughout life. . . . Early learning begets later learning and early success breeds later success. . . . Success or failure at this stage lays the foundation for success or failure in school."

Heckman's point is that the cost of future learning can be reduced by the provision of quality early-childhood experiences. In his words, "The most economically efficient way to remediate the disadvantage caused by adverse family environments is to invest in children when they are young."

I long ago learned that, in policy work, some of a good thing is better than none of that good thing, and I am confident that some pre-K is better than no pre-K. But if all children grow up in a society where programs for 4-year-olds are part of their birthright, as has largely happened with kindergarten, I fear that we may be deluding ourselves. Instead of addressing the underlying problems that too many American children confront early in life, we may have simply transferred those problems to an earlier point in time.

Providing universal access to 4-year-old programs is thought to be the early-education equivalent of creating a level playing field for all children in the year before they enter kindergarten. But this strategy will not result in equity. It won't close the gaps among children of different genetic inheritance, dissimilar financial and familial resources, and disparate early opportunities. Rather, it may have the paradoxical effect of widening the gaps between those with and without advantages in the early years.

Instead of creating similar, across-the-board opportunities in the year before kindergarten, we need to explore how to provide targeted interventions for those who need them most. As has been shown by the state of Illinois, in order to narrow the gap that exists before children arrive at their pre-K programs, we must begin to invest public funds in efforts that start early, provide continuous care, and are comprehensive in terms of services. And to accomplish these goals, we need virtually a Marshall Plan to transform and improve the skills of those working with children from birth to 3 years old.

The start we've made at providing universally available pre-K in this country should not be misrepresented as an example of finished work. We're only partway there.

I am not suggesting that one age group should have pride of place. I, like Professor Bruner, am merely stating the obvious: Well begun is half done. Life doesn't begin at age 4, and solid beginnings are the foundation of later success. The start we've made at providing universally available pre-K in this country should not be misrepresented as an example of finished work. We're only partway there.

We still need to work toward a system of pre-K that takes into account where children begin their journeys through life. To reap the rewards of pre-K, some children will require different kinds of interventions, and some of those interventions will need to be more intense, to be broader in scope, and to begin earlier than is the case for other, more advantaged children.

I concur with the slogan "Pre-K Now." But I'd like to add, "beginning at birth for those who need it most."

. . .

★ CREATING THE BEST
PREKINDERGARTENS ★

*Five Ingredients for Long-Term Effects
and Returns on Investment*

COMMENTARY BY LAWRENCE J. SCHWEINHART
March 19, 2008

STATE-FUNDED PREKINDERGARTEN for 4-year-olds has grown by leaps and bounds in recent years, with the number of such programs up by 40 percent over the last five years alone. One factor contributing to the growth is strong evidence that early-childhood experience influences the development of the brain's architecture. Another is the record of producing beneficial long-term effects and solid returns on investment established by high-quality prekindergarten for children living in low-income families.

The findings come from three major studies of the effects of such programs: the High/Scope Perry Preschool Study, begun by David P. Weikart in 1962; the Carolina Abecedarian Project, begun by Craig T. Ramey in 1972; and the Chicago Child-Parent Centers study, conducted by Arthur J. Reynolds since 1985. These longitudinal studies find strong evidence of the positive effects on participants' intellectual performance in childhood, school achievement in adolescence, placements in regular classes (rather than special education placement or grade retention), high school graduation rate, and adult earnings. They also show fewer teenage births and fewer crimes among participants. Moreover, the economic returns for these programs are from 4 to 16 times as great as the original investments. This extraordinary economic performance is why leading economists, such as the University of Chicago Nobel laureate James J. Heckman, Federal Reserve Chairman Ben S. Bernanke, and others, have publicly embraced these programs.

It is time we explored the differences that make some prekindergartens highly effective, producing a lasting impact on participants' lives, while others are not.

Yet, most recent studies of the federal Head Start program and state-funded prekindergartens have found only modest, short-term effects on children's literacy and social skills and parents' behavior, putting into question whether these programs too can have long-term effects or worthwhile returns on investment. It is time we explored the differences that make some prekindergartens highly effective, producing a lasting impact on participants' lives, while others are not. Five ingredients of the highly effective stand out as definitive, and can serve as rules for how to design such programs:

1. Include children living in low-income families or otherwise at risk of school failure. Long-term effects have seldom been looked for and have yet to be found for children not in these circumstances, although there are arguments for serving them as well. For example, a recent study by William T. Gormley Jr. of Oklahoma's state prekindergartens, which are open to all children, found short-term effects on participants' school achievement that were large enough to promise long-term effects. Prekindergartens open to all children also enjoy a wider political base than a targeted program, and still include the children who are most in need.

2. Have enough qualified teachers and provide them with ongoing support. Qualified teachers are critical to the success of any educational program, a principle now embedded in the federal No

Child Left Behind Act. In early-childhood settings, being qualified is taken to mean having a teaching certificate based on a bachelor's degree in education, child development, or a related field. Because research is constantly informing us about how young children learn and can best be taught, it is also important that early-childhood teachers receive curriculum-based supervision and continuing professional development. Systematic in-service training, in which teachers learn research-based, practical classroom strategies, also helps ensure that young children are having the educational experiences that contribute most to their development.

So that pupils receive sufficient individual attention, highly effective prekindergarten classes have two qualified adults—a teacher and an assistant teacher—for every 16 to 20 4-year-olds. Although having qualified teachers, a low child-to-teacher ratio, and ongoing professional development may cost more, cutting back on these components would threaten program effectiveness as well as the return on investment.

3. Use a validated, interactive child-development curriculum. Such a curriculum enables children as well as teachers to have a hand in designing their own learning activities. It focuses not just on reading and mathematics, but on all aspects of children's development—cognitive, language, social, emotional, motivational, artistic, and physical. And it has evidence of its effectiveness. Implementing such a curriculum requires serious interactive training, study, and practice, particularly for teachers who have little experience with this type of education.

4. Have teachers spend substantial amounts of time with parents, educating them about their children's development and how they can extend classroom learning experiences into their homes. All the programs in the long-term studies worked with parents. In fact, in the High/Scope Perry Preschool program, teachers spent half their work time engaged in such activities. As child care beyond part-day prekindergarten has become more widespread, parent-outreach efforts also need to include other caregivers, in centers and homes, who spend time daily with enrolled children.

5. Confirm results through continuous assessment of program quality and children's development of school readiness. Good curriculum and good assessment go hand in hand. Prekindergartens striving to be highly effective need to replicate the policies and practices of a program found to be highly effective, including the five ingredients listed here. The proof that this is being done lies in program-implementation assessment, a system for measuring how well a program carries out administrative and teaching standards. A program assessor uses standard protocols to observe classrooms and the school, and to interview teachers and others about the various aspects of program quality. The results can then be used for program improvement.

Systematic observation and testing measure prekindergarten children's development of school readiness. With an interactive child-development curriculum, systematic observation fits better than testing, because it records children's usual behavior rather than requiring them to respond on cue in a particular time and place. Program administrators and teachers who know how children are doing on such assessments will be able to use this information to monitor the children's progress and attune their teaching to it.

For the concept of school readiness to contribute to developing highly effective prekindergartens, it must serve as the mediator between prekindergarten and its long-term effects.

Nearly two decades ago, the National Education Goals Panel defined "school readiness" as encompassing not only reading and mathematics, but also other aspects of general knowledge and cognition, physical well-being and motor development, social and emotional development, approaches to learning, and language development. This broad definition also appears in the Head Start Child Outcomes Framework and Canada's Early Development Instrument, an effort in that country and others to assess children's school readiness by having kindergarten teachers rate them on 120 items.

For the concept of school readiness to contribute to developing highly effective prekindergartens, it must serve as the mediator between prekindergarten and its long-term effects. The validity of a school-readiness measure depends on its sensitivity to the effects of prekindergarten and its ability to predict later effects on school achievement and other important life outcomes. In the High/Scope Perry Preschool Study, the program was found to have improved children's intellectual performance and their commitment to schooling, which in turn led to improvements in school achievement, educational attainment, and adult earnings, and to reduced criminal offenses. So in this study, school readiness linking prekindergarten experience and later effects involved motivation as well as intellectual performance.

School readiness so defined could serve as a useful benchmark of the success of today's prekindergartens, guiding them toward both positive long-term effects and good returns on investment.

CHAPTER 2

Reform No Child Left Behind

"These tests shouldn't come at the expense of a well-rounded education—they should help complete that well-rounded education."

BARACK OBAMA

Manchester, N.H., November 20, 2007

THE ISSUE

Although the overall goal of the No Child Left Behind Act (NCLB) is the right one—ensuring that all children can meet high standards—the law has significant flaws that need to be addressed. Barack Obama and Joe Biden believe it was wrong to force teachers, principals, and schools to accomplish the goals of No Child Left Behind without the necessary resources. We have failed to provide high-quality teachers in every classroom and failed to support and pay for those teachers. NCLB must be changed in a fundamental way.

THE OBAMA PLAN

The Obama plan proposals focus on improving NCLB assessment and accountability systems.

- **Improve Assessments:** Obama and Biden believe teachers should not be forced to spend the academic year preparing students to fill in bubbles on standardized tests. They will improve assessments used to track student progress to measure readiness for college and the workplace and improve student learning in a timely, individualized manner.

- **Improve the Accountability System:** Obama and Biden will improve NCLB's accountability system so that we are supporting schools that need improving, rather than punishing them.

CITY LEADERS BACK STRONGER ACCOUNTABILITY

NCLB TESTING SAID TO GIVE 'ILLUSIONS OF PROGRESS'

TOP STUDENTS SAID TO STAGNATE UNDER NCLB

SCHOOLS FOUND LIKELY TO MISS NCLB TARGETS

WHERE'S THE 'CHILD' IN THE NO
CHILD LEFT BEHIND DEBATE?

WHAT TO DO WITH NO CHILD LEFT BEHIND?

. . .

CITY LEADERS BACK STRONGER ACCOUNTABILITY

BY DAVID J. HOFF
July 30, 2008

WASHINGTON. In the debate over the future of the No Child Left Behind Act, many educators say the federal government should ease the law's accountability requirements by setting achievable goals and imposing reasonable sanctions on schools that don't meet them.

But urban leaders—whose schools are most likely to struggle to reach the law's current goals and most apt to face such sanctions—are urging Congress to be more aggressive in holding their schools accountable in the future.

"I think you should make it harder for people like me because it's not about me, it's about my kids," Joel I. Klein, the chancellor of the New York City public schools, told the House Education and Labor Committee at a recent hearing.

The message Mr. Klein and three of his peers gave the panel is consistent with the urban superintendents' stances since President

Bush first proposed linking federal funding to increasing student achievement at the beginning of his administration, said Michael Casserly, the executive director of the Council of the Great City Schools. The Washington group is made up of more than 60 of the country's largest urban districts.

The city schools' group is the only major organization representing educators that lobbied for the NCLB law in 2001 and remains one of its biggest supporters.

"Urban schools are not afraid of accountability," Mr. Casserly said in an interview. "It has helped us focus everyone on student achievement. It's part of the reason why we came out in favor of NCLB in the first place."

Against the Grain

Other groups representing teachers, school board members, and administrators are at odds with the city schools' group.

The law is "too badly broken to be fixed," Randi Weingarten, the new president of the American Federation of Teachers, said in a July 13 speech, the day she was elected to lead the 1.4 million-member union.

Other groups—notably the National School Boards Association and the American Association of School Administrators—are pushing to scale back the student-achievement goals under the law and to give local officials greater discretion when intervening to help struggling schools.

But urban leaders want more, not less, of such accountability. At the July 17 hearing before the House education committee, Mr. Klein and his counterparts from the Atlanta, Chicago, and District of Columbia school systems—as well as the mayors of New York City and Washington—said they want Congress to establish a process to create national academic-content standards and to set up experiments for paying teachers based on the achievement of their students.

Those issues also remain controversial among education groups. Last year's effort to reauthorize the NCLB law stalled when the AFT and the 3.2 million-member National Education Association lobbied against sections of a draft bill that would have created grants to allow districts to base teachers' pay, in part, on the achievement of their students.

Urban leaders are embracing accountability under the NCLB law because it gives them leverage to force changes in schools that otherwise would be resisted by principals and teachers, said Charles L. Glenn, a professor of educational leadership at Boston University.

"It's been remarkable . . . that the bitching and moaning [about accountability] has been coming from the affluent suburbs," he said. But city leaders aren't complaining, he added, "even though they're taking a drubbing" under the federal law's accountability rules.

But many members of urban school boards aren't as enthusiastic as their superintendents about the law's accountability measures, said Reginald M. Felton, the director of federal relations for the NSBA, which is based in Alexandria, Va.

"They have felt they are at a disadvantage in how [the NCLB law] measures accountability," Mr. Felton said in describing a common view among school board members. "Most of the discussion [over accountability] has been about how to be fair about how you measure progress and achievement."

NCLB on Hold

Although the House panel called the city leaders to the recent hearing, the ideas discussed won't become law anytime soon. With so much attention focused on the presidential campaign and pressing economic concerns, Congress has postponed debate over the future of the NCLB law, leaving it for the next president and members of the next Congress to decide.

But the urban superintendents' statements reinforced the message that there's no consensus among educators over whether the NCLB law—which requires schools to make annual progress toward raising all students to proficiency in reading and math—has helped schools improve, or on what changes would fix the law's flaws.

The divisions among educators over accountability, national standards and tests, and teacher pay will likely remain hard to bridge once Congress resumes trying to reauthorize the NCLB law, which is the latest version of the Elementary and Secondary Education Act of 1965.

National standards and tests would make it easier for educators to know how the achievement of their students compares with the performance of the rest of the country, the urban leaders said at the hearing.

"The fact that you have 50 different hurdles for our children to jump over, that doesn't make any sense," Arne Duncan, the chief executive officer of the 408,000-student Chicago school system, said at the hearing.

"We need to have national standards and national assessments, so then everybody can understand that if you're proficient in math in California, you're proficient in math in New York," added Mr. Klein of the 1.1 million-student New York City system.

Democrats on the House panel questioned whether it would be fair to require all students to meet national standards if some attend schools that are inadequately financed.

"When we talk about national standards, that's great. But what about the inequity in funding?" said Rep. Donald M. Payne, D-N.J., who represents Newark.

But the urban leaders responded that national standards would show how low student achievement is linked to inadequate spending and would buttress arguments that money needs to be redistributed from affluent areas to poor ones.

"If we went to national standards," Mr. Duncan said, "that would force the conversation about funding inequities that we skirt now."

Paying for Performance

Another Democrat on the committee questioned the feasibility of devising teacher-compensation systems tied to students' achievement on tests.

It would be difficult to create a system that is "fair and objective and defensible," said Rep. Lynn Woolsey of California. "That's what it's going to take to get all teachers to buy in to what will be in their best interests in the long run."

Finding a way to do that is important even though "there's an incredible amount of pushback to this," said Michelle A. Rhee, the chancellor of the 50,000-student District of Columbia public schools.

Many proposals would increase the pay of teachers who take jobs in schools where student achievement is lowest, but Ms. Rhee argued that such teachers need to be further rewarded if they succeed in improving achievement in those schools.

"It'd be incredibly important for the Democratic Party to step up on this," she said.

.   .   .

NCLB TESTING SAID TO GIVE 'ILLUSIONS OF PROGRESS'

BY SCOTT J. CECH
September 28, 2008

HARVARD UNIVERSITY RESEARCHER Daniel M. Koretz had some good news and some bad news today for policymakers looking ahead to the reauthorization of the federal No Child Left Behind Act: The nation's K–12 students are now attending Lake Wobegon schools.

That is, he said, for reasons that are politically better but academically worse, rampantly inflated standardized test scores are giving the misbegotten impression that, as in the fictional town made famous by radio personality Garrison Keillor, all children are above average.

"We know that we are creating, in many cases, with our test-based accountability system, illusions of progress," Mr. Koretz told a roomful of policymakers and educators at a panel discussion here hosted by the American Enterprise Institute, a Washington think tank.

Mr. Koretz, a professor of education at Harvard Graduate School of Education who has written a new book, *Measuring Up: What Edu-*

cational Testing Really Tells Us, added that under the No Child Left Behind law, widespread teaching to the test, strategic reallocation of teaching talent, and other means of gaming the high-stakes testing system have conspired to produce scores on state standardized tests that are substantially better than students' mastery of the material.

"If you tell people that performance on that tested sample is what matters, that's what they worry about, so you can get inappropriate responses in the classroom and inflated test scores," he said, citing research in the 1990s on the state standardized test then

---

No Child Left Behind

The No Child Left Behind (NCLB) Act of 2001, signed into law by President Bush on January 8, 2002, is a reauthorization of the Elementary and Secondary Education Act, the central federal law in precollegiate education. The ESEA, first enacted in 1965 and reauthorized a total of eight times as of 2008, includes Title I, the federal government's flagship aid program for disadvantaged students. The act's Title III is the conduit for most federal funding for English-language-learner programs.

As the newest incarnation of the ESEA, the No Child Left Behind Act has expanded the federal role in education and become a focal point of education policy. Coming at a time of wide public concern about the state of education, the legislation sets in place requirements that reach into virtually every public school in America. It takes particular aim at improving the educational lot of disadvantaged students. NCLB centers on numerous measures designed to improve achievement and accountability in schools, including ensuring that schools are making what is termed "adequate yearly progress" in student achievement and employing teachers deemed to be "highly qualified." NCLB mandates that states test students in reading and mathematics in Grades 3–8 and once in high school, ranking them as either advanced, proficient, basic, or below basic. Under the law, all students must be proficient in those subjects by the 2013–14 school year.

From The Education Week Guide to K–12 Terminology

---

in use in Kentucky, which was designed to measure similar aspects of proficiency as the National Assessment of Educational Progress, often called "the nation's report card."

Scores on both tests should have moved more or less in lock step, he said. But instead, 4th grade reading scores rose dramatically on the state test, which in many ways resembled an NCLB-test prototype, from 1992 to 1994, while sliding slightly on the NAEP over the same period.

"If you're a parent in Kentucky, what you care about is whether your kids can read, not how well they can do on the state test," Mr. Koretz said. "And the national assessment told us that in fact the gains in the state test were bogus."

Obscuring or Illuminating?

Bella Rosenberg, an education consultant and a longtime special assistant to the American Federation of Teachers' late president, Albert Shanker, echoed many of Mr. Koretz's critiques.

"This is officially sanctioned malpractice—if we did this in health, in medical practice, we'd all be dead by now," she said of the testing system under the NCLB law. "The fact is, we're doing a great job of obscuring instead of illuminating achievement gaps."

But fellow panelist Roberto Rodriguez, a senior education adviser to U.S. Sen. Edward M. Kennedy, D-Mass., the chairman of the Senate Health, Education, Labor, and Pensions Committee who helped shepherd the NCLB law through Congress in 2001, cautioned against "throwing the baby out with the bath water."

While a more effective accountability system "needs to be a goal, I would argue, of the upcoming reauthorization of the ESEA," he said, referring to the Elementary and Secondary Education Act, which is now known as NCLB, "summative assessment is a critically important area of accountability."

With regard to the tug-of-war between advocates of the current standards-based system and detractors who prefer a system that better reflects the curriculum, Mr. Rodriguez said, "I think we can have our cake and eat it too."

Williamson M. Evers, the U.S. Department of Education's assistant secretary for planning, evaluation, and policy development, who attended the panel discussion, suggested that any changes to the NCLB law should preserve its essence. "Some are proposing changes in accountability that remove consequences; this would make it accountability in name only," Mr. Evers said in an e-mail. "Results should be comparable statewide, or parents, taxpayers, and teachers themselves can't tell how students are doing."

. . .

TOP STUDENTS SAID TO
STAGNATE UNDER NCLB

BY DEBRA VIADERO
June 18, 2008

WHILE THE NATION'S poorest-performing students have made academic progress under the federal No Child Left Behind Act, the brightest students appear to be languishing for lack of attention, according to a report released today by a Washington think tank.

"People have been complaining ever since NCLB passed that focusing resources on the bottom students would come at the expense of high-achieving students," said Tom Loveless, one of the authors of the report. "There hasn't been any Robin Hood effect, but the high achievers haven't been gaining, either."

Titled "High-Achieving Students in the Era of NCLB," the report from the Thomas B. Fordham Foundation draws on national test-score data and results from a nationwide survey of 900 public school teachers in grades 3–12 to paint a portrait of a generation of high achievers left to fend for themselves as schools and teachers shift their time and resources toward educational strategies aimed more at bringing the bottom up than on raising achievement for all children.

The data show, for instance, that from 2000 to 2007, the scores of the top 10 percent of students essentially held steady on National

Assessment of Educational Progress tests in reading and math. The scores for the bottom 10 percent of students, meanwhile, rose by 18 points on the 4th grade reading test and 13 points in 8th grade math—the equivalent of about a year's worth of learning by Mr. Loveless' calculations. (One exception to that pattern was in 8th grade reading, where low-achieving students' scores declined and the achievement gap widened slightly.)

What's difficult to tell is whether the disparity was caused by the federal law or whether it reflects longer-term educational trends. The legislation, which was signed into law in 2002, imposes consequences on schools for failing to improve the scores of low-achieving students.

"We would make the argument that NCLB is linked to state standards, and some state standards are not terribly high, so maybe one of the problems for the high-achieving kids is that there isn't enough stretch for them," said Amy Wilkins, the vice president for governmental affairs and communications for the Education Trust, a Washington-based group that promotes educational equity and is supportive of the federal law.

Roots in the 1990s

A handful of studies in recent years have examined the 6-year-old law's impact on students who are academically struggling, on the "bubble kids" who fall just below passing levels on state tests, and on poor and minority students. Yet few—if any—have focused on academically advanced students.

The new report combines findings from the first two of five planned reports from the Fordham Foundation on the educational status of children at the high end of the academic spectrum. The Washington-based research organization advocates high academic standards and is a prominent supporter of charter schools.

To some extent, the narrowing of the achievement gap that occurred in the post-NCLB years had its start in the 1990s, according to Mr. Loveless, who is a senior fellow at the Brookings Institution and director of its Brown Center on Education Policy. During those years, the gains made by low-achieving students outpaced those of top achievers and then began to accelerate after 2000.

The gains for low achievers were most pronounced, however, in states that had begun to put in place accountability systems similar to that of NCLB's. In those states, Mr. Loveless found, test scores improved for the bottom 10 percent of students at a faster clip than they did for the top 10 percent. The academic gains for the latter group began to slow after states imposed new high-stakes testing systems.

"We can't say that NCLB 'caused' the achievement of the nation's top students to stagnate, any more than it 'caused' the achievement of our lowest-performing students to rise dramatically," the report says. "All we know is that the acceleration in achievement gains by low-performing students is associated with the introduction of NCLB (and, earlier, with state accountability systems)."

Teachers' Take

According to results from surveys and focus-group interviews conducted as part of the study, teachers seemed to agree that the federal law had negative consequences for their best-performing students.

Eighty-one percent of teachers, for example, said low-achieving students are most likely to get one-on-one attention from teachers, while only 5 percent named advanced students as the group that drew the most individual attention.

Likewise, 73 percent of teachers agreed that "too often, the brightest students are bored and underchallenged in school."

More than three-quarters of teachers—77 percent—agreed that "getting underachieving students to reach 'proficiency' has become so important that the needs of advanced students take a back seat."

"I had expected public school teachers to say that it was far more important to raise the achievement of low-performing kids, and they said equity means that no group of students should be neglected," said Steve Farkas, the president of the New York City-based Farkas Duffett Research Group and the co-author of that part of the report.

Teachers also expressed concern about being inadequately trained to teach advanced students or to differentiate their instruction so that all students make progress in classrooms with students of mixed academic abilities.

Nancy Green, the executive director of the Washington-based National Association for Gifted Children, said the findings fit with the anecdotal reports that she gets from teachers and parents of gifted children.

"You get what you measure," she said. "Given that we're getting beaten over the head over issues of the U.S.'s [economic] competitiveness now, we're wondering how long it will be before policymakers make the connection between the needs of gifted kids and national competitiveness."

The top-ranking students tended, for the most part, to be white students from the suburbs. But Mr. Loveless also analyzed data on the small subgroups of African-American, Hispanic, and low-income students in their ranks. In 8th grade math, for instance, he found that high achievers from those groups were more likely than low achievers to be taught by experienced teachers. They were also just as likely as other high achievers to have teachers with regular teaching licenses or with undergraduate majors or minors in math, findings that echo other recent research highlighting the importance of high-quality teaching.

· · ·

SCHOOLS FOUND LIKELY TO MISS NCLB TARGETS

BY SEAN CAVANAGH AND DAVID J. HOFF
October 1, 2008

TWO NEW STUDIES cast doubt on U.S. schools' ability to make the academic improvements required under the No Child Left Behind Act, a topic likely to be of prime concern to members of Congress next year as it prepares to review the law's core goals during reauthorization.

One study probes a central tenet of the nearly 7-year-old federal law: that all students will reach academic proficiency by the 2013–14 school year, a goal viewed as unrealistic by many policymakers and observers.

Using statistical-modeling techniques, the study's authors examine the progress of the nation's most populous state, California, in attempting to meet the proficiency mark. They conclude that nearly all the state's elementary schools will fail to meet that target, in large part because of the difficulty of bringing English-language learners and economically disadvantaged students up to speed academically.

The study, published this week in the scholarly journal *Science*, focuses only on California. But its analysis of the difficulty of reaching proficiency could probably apply to other states that have adopted similar strategies and timelines for making progress toward the 2013–14 proficiency goal, said Richard A. Cardullo, a professor of biology at the University of California, Riverside, who is one of the authors.

Problems Obscured

Recent increases in the statewide percentage of California students' reaching the "proficient" or "advanced" level on state tests tend to obscure the difficulty that individual schools have in meeting the goals of the federal law, the authors say. Subgroups of students in those schools, particularly English-language learners and disadvantaged students, are likely to continue to struggle to meet the federal mandate over the next five years, the study concludes.

"Redirecting the focus to the lowest-performing subgroups at each school results in a different distribution in school performance," the authors say, which "reveals a profound acceleration in the [rate] at which schools will fail to make AYP," or adequate yearly progress.

A team of researchers at UC-Riverside completed the study. They are working on a project, financed with a $5 million grant from the National Science Foundation and directed by Mr. Cardullo, that examines strategies for improving student achievement and teacher training in mathematics.

The NCLB law requires schools to test students annually in grades 3–8 and once in high school in reading and math, and make adequate yearly progress in those subjects.

While many observers agree that schools will not meet the NCLB law's goal of universal proficiency by 2013–14, states are required to hold schools accountable for meeting achievement targets based on that goal.

Stuck in Restructuring

That is one of the reasons there has been a significant rise in the number of schools entering the law's "restructuring" phase, according to a second study, released this week by the Center on Education Policy, a Washington think thank.

That study, "A Call to Restructure Restructuring: Lessons from the No Child Left Behind Act in Five States," estimates that during the 2007–08 school year, 3,599 schools nationwide were forced to choose one of several restructuring options to change their management or instructional strategies with the goal of improving student performance.

The number represents a 56 percent increase from the year before, according to the report by the center, a research and policy group that is tracking the federal law's implementation. Schools are required to undergo restructuring if they fail to make adequate yearly progress—the measure of whether they are on pace to meet the law's achievement goal—for five years.

The two studies have emerged as Congress prepares to consider proposals to reauthorize the No Child Left Behind Act, though interest in the topic has waned in recent months as attention to the ongoing presidential and congressional campaigns has increased.

Some supporters of the law, such as U.S. Secretary of Education Margaret Spellings, have argued that the 2013–14 proficiency goal should be kept intact. Relaxing that goal would lessen schools' incentive to improve academically, they argue.

Others, however, have suggested postponing the deadline or modifying the proficiency target. Even some of the law's biggest supporters agree that it will be virtually impossible to achieve universal proficiency by the end of the 2013–14 school year.

The main reason is that schools failed to comply with the NCLB law's mandate to hire "highly qualified" teachers in schools serving disadvantaged students, said Amy Wilkins, the vice president of governmental affairs and communications for the Education Trust, a Washington-based research and advocacy group that was instrumental in designing the law, which Congress passed in December 2001.

"We haven't provided the help to struggling schools, and we haven't provided the teachers they need," said Ms. Wilkins. "Good teachers dramatically change not just the learning trajectories, but the life trajectories of students, and we didn't do that."

Last year, the Education Trust proposed extending the deadline for states that agreed to revise their proficiency standards and gear them toward preparing students for college or the workforce.

Tough Standard for States?

The California study found that for most of the state's elementary schools, the greatest difficulty in meeting the 2013–14 proficiency deadline will come in language arts rather than math. Disadvantaged students and those with limited English skills are most likely to cause schools to miss the mark, and the data suggest that "very little change in this pattern can be anticipated over the next five years," the authors conclude.

The study's findings are disappointing but not surprising, said Hilary McLean, a spokeswoman for California schools superintendent Jack O'Connell. He has asked federal officials for changes that will give the state credit for improving student performance, particularly among struggling learners, she said.

"Unless states are willing to water down their standards—which we're not—you're going to see this pattern replicated in other states," Ms. McLean said.

The Center on Education Policy study, which examines school results in California, Georgia, Maryland, Michigan, and Ohio, found that once struggling schools go into mandatory restructuring, it's hard for them to exit.

In the 2007–08 school year, for example, just 19 percent of the restructuring schools met their AYP goals. Schools must meet those goals for two consecutive years to break out of the NCLB law's accountability interventions.

As the 2013–14 school year nears, it will become more difficult for all schools to meet their AYP goals, which are escalating based on meeting the proficiency goal by the end of that time frame, one of the report's authors says.

"States are anticipating more and more schools being in the later stages of restructuring," said Caitlin Scott, the lead researcher for the CEP report.

. . .

★ WHERE'S THE 'CHILD' IN THE NO CHILD LEFT BEHIND DEBATE? ★

COMMENTARY BY THOMAS E. PETRI
February 4, 2008

LISTENING TO RECENT DEBATES in Congress and on the presidential campaign trail regarding the reauthorization of the federal No Child Left Behind Act, one might wonder where the aforementioned "child" is.

Merit pay, professional development, and supplementary educational services are just a few of the hotly contested issues. And all sides appear to be entrenched, with little hope of reconciliation this year.

As important as these issues are, they are ultimately peripheral to the individual students and the impact this law has had on them. Frankly, too little attention has been paid to the "child" that the law was designed to serve.

In enacting this law, Congress placed new and significant demands on students and teachers in the form of mandatory state standards and assessments to track progress toward meeting NCLB goals. With its strong accountability mechanisms, the 2002 law represented a landmark change in federal education policy.

But the current reauthorization process has scarcely focused on why and how we administer these assessments and what value they provide to individual educators and students.

The most important changes Congress should make are, in fact, those that have quietly been agreed to, and in some cases implemented, by the U.S. Department of Education on an administrative basis. Amid the acrimony surrounding the law's reauthorization, we've lost sight of the fact that there are many changes we can agree on—and these would have the greatest direct impact on the nation's students.

Amid the acrimony surrounding the law's reauthorization, we've lost sight of the fact that there are many changes we can agree on.

One example of a consensus change is the move toward greater use of "growth models," which track individual student improvement rather than look at a class as a static snapshot. The Education Department has learned, and Congress has quietly concurred, that growth models using robust computer systems that track student progress from year to year are far better mechanisms for gauging individual student growth and ensuring accountability for improvement.

Another area where parties seem to have reached consensus is in reforming school restructuring programs, which apply to schools that do not make adequate yearly progress in student performance over a period of several years. Failure of a school to make adequate progress over a number of years results in strict intervention, which is important. These restructuring programs, however, may be wasted on schools that are only slightly missing targets, rather than failing on a widespread basis. We can all agree to restructuring reform that focuses resources on the schools that need them most, without wasting taxpayers' money on schools that are otherwise on target, save for a small category of students.

Finally, one of the most common and valid complaints under the existing version of NCLB is that the kinds of state tests mandated under the law are largely worthless from the perspective of students, teachers, and parents. Those tests measure the schools, but are far too long in processing and far too limited in scope to tell much about how individual students are performing.

One simple change that is gaining broad support would allow states to choose to use computer adaptive testing, rather than an archaic paper test, for their statewide assessments under NCLB.

Computer adaptive assessments adjust automatically as the student takes the test. If the student is doing well, the test asks harder questions. If the student is having difficulty, the questions get easier. The result is a highly personalized assessment that is reported on a scale common to all students. In other words, an adaptive assessment can provide an accurate measure of a child's skills and abilities, while also measuring grade-level performance.

It's time to set the heated rhetoric of special interests
aside and pass a set of pragmatic changes.

Congress should give all states the flexibility to use adaptive testing to determine grade-level achievement and also to provide student-growth data that teachers can use to help students learn to the best of their abilities. With adaptive testing in place, parents and teachers can be better informed in order to help each child meet grade-level expectations through a realistic academic plan. U.S. Rep. David Wu, D-Ore., and I have introduced a bill to give states this flexibility.

Setting aside the other "hotly contested issues," there are a myriad of technical and consensus provisions Congress could pass this year that President Bush should be comfortable signing into law. We can make important adjustments that will make the law work better for students, while preserving the strong accountability standards currently in place.

It's time to set the heated rhetoric of special interests aside and pass a set of pragmatic changes this year that can better make this law work for students who, after all, are supposed to be our primary concern.

. . .

★ # WHAT TO DO WITH NO CHILD LEFT BEHIND? ★

Why the Law Will Need More Than a Name Change

COMMENTARY BY RICHARD D. KAHLENBERG
October 15, 2008

FOLLOWING THE ELECTION, a new president and Congress will need to sit down and figure out what to do with President Bush's signature piece of domestic legislation, the No Child Left Behind Act. The first order of business will be to come up with a new name. U.S. Rep. George Miller, D-Calif., an architect of the legislation, has quipped that the NCLB brand has become so toxic that simply changing the name would pick up 100 votes for the legislation.

But then comes the hard work: fixing a law that has grown unpopular not only with those who have opposed standards, testing, and accountability all along, but also with supporters of standards-based reform who recognize that NCLB has taken the idea off track.

Originally, standards-based reform was driven by the idea that there was a big hole at the center of American education: a lack of agreement on what skills and knowledge students should master. Expectations varied widely between schools, and there was little outside pressure for anyone in the system—students, teachers, or principals—to work very hard.

In their influential 1991 paper "Systemic School Reform," Marshall S. Smith and Jennifer O'Day suggested an alternative to this chaos: the establishment of standards, which would guide curriculum, testing, and teacher training and development. Standards-based reform also envisioned consequences for failing schools, including the right of students stuck in bad schools to transfer to better-performing ones. Many advocates of standards-based reform also recognized that asking schools to do what had never been done before—educating all students to high levels—would require substantially greater funding.

Although the No Child Left Behind Act was an outgrowth of the standards-based reform movement, it departs in significant ways from the movement's early ideals. Scholars in the field have proposed solutions to three central defects in the legislation—the underfunding of NCLB; the flawed implementation of its standards, testing, and accountability provisions; and the failure to provide students in low-performing schools a genuine opportunity to transfer to much better ones—in a recently released book, *Improving on No Child Left Behind*, which I edited. Here are some of their recommendations:

Funding

To date, most of the debate over the funding of No Child Left Behind has pitted Democrats, who point to the gap between authorized levels of funding and appropriations (which reached $70.9 billion by fiscal 2008), against Republicans, who respond that authorization levels provide a ceiling that is typically not met by appropriations. The discussion avoids the fundamental question: What is the true cost of NCLB's goal of making all students academically proficient by 2014?

Federal funding would have to multiply many times over to help districts succeed in meeting even the intermediate goals of the legislation.

According to new research in the book, detailed by authors William Duncombe and John Yinger of Syracuse University and

Anna Lukemeyer of the University of Nevada, Las Vegas, federal funding would have to multiply many times over to help districts succeed in meeting even the intermediate goals of the legislation. They note that the costs of reaching 90 percent proficiency (short of the law's ultimate goal of 100 percent proficiency) will vary from state to state, depending upon the level of performance standard adopted, the local cost of living, and the demographic makeup of the student population. But based on a careful review of historical data on the relationship between spending and performance, and looking at four representative states, the researchers find that even if states increased funding by 15 percent and districts became 15 percent more efficient at spending resources (ambitious goals), federal Title I aid would have to be increased by 18 percent in Kansas, 129 percent in New York state, 547 percent in California, and a whopping 1,077 percent in Missouri to meet the goal of 90 percent student proficiency.

Standards, Testing, and Accountability

A coherent system of standards, testing, and accountability was to be the hallmark of standards-based reform, but as Lauren Resnick, Mary Kay Stein, and Sarah Coon of the University of Pittsburgh write in their chapter, the No Child Left Behind law is marked by myriad problems: the failure of states to develop clear and rigorous content standards for what students should know and be able to do; the poor quality of most state assessments that makes "teaching to the test" a big problem rather than a desired outcome; the varying state-by-state performance standards; the adoption of an arbitrary single standard of proficiency that is too high for some students with disabilities, and not high enough for gifted pupils; the incentive to focus most heavily on students who are on the cusp of becoming proficient, to the detriment of those far below or above the bar; and the failure to isolate the effects of family and the effects of school on student achievement.

Moreover, unlike the original vision for standards-based reform, the No Child Left Behind law contains only sticks and no carrots, the authors argue, creating a compliance mentality among teachers rather than spurring efforts to enhance student learning.

What is to be done? Establish clear and well-defined standards, set at the national level if possible, or by a small number of state consortia. Produce high-quality tests that are linked to these standards. Abolish the ludicrous goal of 100 percent proficiency to a single standard and, instead, set multiple standards with the goal of moving all segments of the distribution up at least one notch. Use well-constructed, value-added models of achievement that better measure what children are learning in school, as opposed to what they have learned before kindergarten or during summers off. And use carrots as well as sticks as incentives for students and teachers alike.

What is to be done? Establish clear and well-defined standards, set at the national level if possible.

Student Transfers

The federal law has broken its promise to provide low-income students stuck in failing schools the opportunity to attend much-better-performing schools, because urban districts typically have very few good schools available to receive these students. As Amy Stuart Wells of Teachers College, Columbia University, and Jennifer Jellison Holme of the University of Texas at Austin explain in their chapter, to fix this problem NCLB should provide financial incentives to encourage high-performing suburban schools to accept transfers by low-income urban students.

Wells and Holme examine interdistrict integration programs in eight communities—Boston; East Palo Alto, Calif.; Hartford, Conn.; Indianapolis; Milwaukee; Minneapolis; Rochester, N.Y.; and St. Louis—and conclude that carefully designed student-transfer programs can produce extraordinary outcomes for students. They find that low-income minority students can perform at high levels if given the right environment, but that NCLB's current efforts—trying to make "separate but equal" work—are far less promising than programs providing low-income students a genuine opportunity to attend economically and racially integrated schools.

Failing to address the three central flaws of No Child Left Behind could undermine the standards-based reform movement—and indeed, our entire system of public education. Critics of standards-based reform have always feared that the program was designed to facilitate privatization, and NCLB's flawed system in many ways does set public schools up for failure. It requires 100 percent student proficiency without providing adequate resources. It fails to establish a coherent and sophisticated set of standards and assessments, and it holds schools accountable for factors beyond their control. And by failing to provide urban children stuck in under-performing schools with access to suburban schools, it plays into the argument that only private school vouchers can meet the demand for choice.

Failing to address the three central flaws of No Child Left Behind could undermine the standards-based reform movement— and indeed, our entire system of public education.

On the other hand, if standards-based reform is put back on track, it will drown out the wrongheaded calls for privatization. A well-constructed reauthorization bill—one that fully funded the ambitious goals of NCLB; provided coherent national standards tied to high-quality assessments and reasonable stakes for students and teachers; and included a genuine transfer option for low-income students to attend high-quality, middle-class suburban schools—would strengthen America's public education system immeasurably.

CHAPTER 3

Expand Choice and Innovation

"I want to lead a new era of mutual responsibility in education—
one where we all come together for the sake of our children's
success; an era where each of us does our part to make that
success a reality—parents and teachers, leaders in Washington,
and citizens all across America."

BARACK OBAMA

Manchester, N.H., November 20, 2007

THE ISSUE

*Public education in America should foster innovation and
provide students with varied, high-quality learning opportunities.
Unfortunately, while there are many examples of individual
school success, there are still too many barriers to replicating
educational excellence on a larger scale. It's time to focus
resources on the most effective programs with a proven record
of success, and work to expand successful school choices for
parents and students within public education.*

THE OBAMA PLAN

The Obama-Biden plan includes proposals to:

- **Create an Innovative Schools Program:** Help states and school districts implement plans to create a "portfolio" of successful public school types, including charters, nonprofit schools, Montessori schools, career academies, and theme-focused schools.

- **Support High-Quality Schools and Close Low-Performing Charter Schools:** Double funding for the Federal Charter School Program to support the creation of more successful charter schools. The Obama-Biden administration will provide this expanded charter school funding only to states that improve accountability for charter schools, allow for interventions in struggling charter schools, and have a clear process for closing down chronically underperforming charter schools. Obama and Biden will also prioritize supporting states that help the most successful charter schools to expand to serve more students.

- **Enlist Parents and Communities to Support Teaching and Learning:** Call on parents, families, and schools to work together and take responsibility for instilling in young people our best shared values like honesty, hard work, and preparation for good citizenship.

PERSPECTIVES

EDGE SEEN FOR CHICAGO CHARTER HIGH SCHOOLS

NAEP GAP CONTINUING FOR CHARTERS

'GREEN' CHARTERS FORGE A NETWORK

GAINS FOR A NEW ORLEANS CHARTER SCHOOL

A DEFINING MOMENT FOR CHARTER SCHOOLS?

FEDERAL EDUCATION INNOVATION — GETTING IT RIGHT

. . .

EDGE SEEN FOR CHICAGO CHARTER HIGH SCHOOLS

*Graduation and College-Going Rates
Higher than Regular Public Schools'*

BY DEBRA VIADERO
May 14, 2008

A FIRST-OF-ITS-KIND analysis suggests that in Chicago, at least, charter school students are more likely to graduate from high school and enroll in college than similar students in regular public high schools.

Released May 7 by researchers from the RAND Corp., Mathematica, and Florida State University in Tallahassee, the study is the first in the nation to track high school outcomes for students enrolled in charter schools. It finds that attending a charter high school in that city boosts a student's chance of graduating from high school by 7 percentage points and increases the likelihood that a student will enroll in college by 11 percentage points.

But it also finds that, at the elementary and middle school level, students in Chicago's charter schools don't appear to make any greater learning gains than their peers in regular public schools.

"The bottom line is that the attainment effects that we're seeing are very promising and quite substantial, and they're going to be important for not only policy but for future research on charter schools," said Brian P. Gill, a study co-author and a senior social scientist at the Princeton, N.J.-based Mathematica Policy Research Inc.

Numbering more than 4,000 across the nation, charter schools are public schools that are allowed to operate with fewer of the bureaucratic constraints that apply to most regular public schools.

In the 408,000-student Chicago school system, charters serve an estimated 20,000 students in 28 schools, with two more such schools scheduled to open in the fall. The rapid growth of charters in that city is due in part to its 4-year-old Renaissance 2010 initiative, which seeks to create 100 new schools by 2010.

Part of Larger Project

The Chicago findings are among the first to emerge from a larger project looking at the growth of charter schools in four cities—Chicago, Milwaukee, Philadelphia, and San Diego—and in the states of Florida, Ohio, and Texas. It's being underwritten by the Seattle-based Bill & Melinda Gates Foundation, the Joyce Foundation in Chicago, the Stranahan Foundation in Toledo, Ohio, and the William Penn Foundation in Philadelphia.

One of the stickiest problems in research comparing charter schools with regular public schools is how to account for the fact that charter school students might be more motivated to learn because they—or their families—choose the schools they attend.

To get around that problem, the researchers in the Chicago study compared the achievement trajectories for the same students before and after they switched to charter schools. In keeping with other studies on charter schools, the researchers found that students make similar learning gains in reading and mathematics in both types of schools in grades 3 through 8.

The study also found that, both in terms of student achievement and in terms of their racial and ethnic mix, the charter schools to which students transferred looked no different than the traditional schools they left behind.

"That's important because there's been a debate about whether charter schools are cream-skimming kids from traditional public schools or contributing to racial stratification," said Ron Zimmer, another study co-author and a senior policy researcher at the Santa Monica, Calif.-based RAND Corp.

The study's main innovation, though, is its high school analysis. For that part of the study, researchers control for potential biases by focusing on a subset of about 1,000 students who attended charter schools in 8th grade and then went on to either a traditional public high school or remained in the same charter school. (The grade configurations available to Chicago charter school students include schools serving students in grades 7–12, 6–12, or K–12.)

Unusual Analysis

In 8th grade, Mr. Gill said, both groups were similar in terms of demographics and achievement levels. But the students who stayed in charter schools went on to earn higher scores on college-entrance exams and graduate from high school and enroll in college at higher rates than their counterparts in traditional high schools.

On the ACT college-entrance tests, the charter school students scored, on average, half a point higher than their traditional-school counterparts. (That's in an analysis for which the median score was 16, out of a possible 36, according to Mr. Gill.)

"What we have to acknowledge here, though," added Mr. Gill, "is that it's possible that the positive effects we're seeing could be a result of the grade configuration itself. It could be that kids benefit from eliminating the transition that kids make from middle school to high school."

District school officials also acknowledged that the city's charter high schools are typically smaller than its traditional high schools, many of which enroll 1,000 or more students. On the other hand, the study notes, those schools may have unconventional grade configurations or smaller enrollments because they are charters.

Independent experts praised the study for its rigor. Whether the findings will apply more generally to charter high schools in other states, though, remains an open question, they said. "Every charter school reform gets a different character," said Gary W. Miron, an education professor at Western Michigan University in Kalamazoo.

Charter high schools in Connecticut, for example, provide a more remedial function, he noted. In Delaware, they focus on college preparation. "But we need to get beyond student achievement alone in these kinds of evaluations," Mr. Miron said, "and this is one of the few studies that do that."

Preliminary findings from the larger multistate study do suggest that a similar pattern of high school attainment for charter schools is emerging in Florida.

Chicago school officials said they weren't surprised by the positive findings. District data, however, shows charter school pupils at the elementary level outscoring the district average. The results differ because the district report, also released last week, gives a

---

Charter Schools

Charter schools run independently of the traditional public school system but receive public funding. In exchange for regulatory freedom, the schools are bound to the terms of a contract or "charter" that lays out their mission, academic goals, and accountability procedures. State laws set the parameters for charter contracts, which are overseen by a designated charter school authorizer— often the local school district or related agency.

With their relative autonomy, charter schools are seen as a way to provide greater educational choice and innovation within the public school system. Their founders are often teachers, parents, or activists who feel restricted by traditional public schools. In addition, many charters are run by for-profit companies, forming a key component of the privatization movement in education. The first charter school was founded in Minnesota in 1992.

From The Education Week Guide to K–12 Terminology

---

snapshot of student performance on 2006–07 tests rather than tracking achievement growth over time.

. . .

NAEP GAP CONTINUING FOR CHARTERS

Sector's Scores Lag in Three Out of Four Main Categories

BY ERIK W. ROBELEN

May 21, 2008

NEARLY FOUR YEARS after a front-page story in the *New York Times* sparked a fierce debate by suggesting that charter school students nationally were lagging academically behind their peers in regular public schools, the national testing program that informed the controversy has generated far more data for researchers and advocates to scrutinize.

Yet the more recent findings from the National Assessment of Educational Progress have garnered much less attention and analysis than the 2003 results.

The picture that emerges from the growing data set appears mixed for charter schools. While many analysts urge caution in using NAEP to judge the 4,300-school charter sector, the latest data do not bolster the early hopes of charter advocates that the sector as a whole would significantly outperform regular public schools.

The overall scores of charter students tested in 2007 in the nationally representative assessment program were lower than for students in regular public schools in 4th grade reading and mathematics, and in 8th grade math, all by statistically significant margins.

In 4th grade reading, charter students had an average score of 214, compared with 220 for regular public schools, on a 500-point scale. Looked at another way, 59 percent of charter students scored at or above the "basic" reading level on the NAEP test, compared with 66 percent in other public schools.

But in 8th grade reading, charter students appeared to essentially close a gap from 2005, with charter and regular public school students scoring about the same in 2007.

Digging deeper in the data reveals a more complex story, though limited sample sizes for charter schools make many score differences hard to interpret with confidence. For low-income black students—a key population served by many urban charters—the 2007 performance gaps between charter and noncharter schools generally appeared smaller than those between the two sectors' populations as a whole, and none was large enough to be deemed statistically significant.

Hispanic charter students, meanwhile, appeared to do about as well as or better than their peers in regular public schools across grades and subjects. But here, too, limited sample sizes make the differences too small to state with confidence.

Piece of the Puzzle

Researchers emphasize that because of NAEP's design, the program has serious limitations in assessing charter schools, or comparing them with other public schools. Some experts argue that the tests are altogether ill-suited for the purpose.

The congressionally mandated NAEP—known as "the nation's report card"—provides a snapshot of performance at a single point in time, testing different students each cycle. It also does not take into account prior achievement.

Even with those and other caveats, some researchers—though not all—suggest the results are a useful part of the growing research base on charter achievement.

"I personally don't believe we're going to have a single, definitive study to tell us whether charters are working," said Gary J. Miron, a principal research associate at the evaluation center at Western Michigan University, who studies charter schools. "The NAEP is one more piece of the puzzle. . . . And now we have multiple snapshots."

The debate over charter schools and NAEP first came to public prominence following an August 2004 story in the *New York*

Times. The article focused on an analysis conducted by the American Federation of Teachers, which had called for a national moratorium on new charter schools in 2002.

The AFT study used reading and math scores in 2003, the first time charter students' NAEP scores were reported separately. It concluded that charter students trailed those in regular public schools as a whole, and also when results were broken down by such subgroups as black students or students eligible for free or reduced-price lunches.

The report and news story spurred an outcry from charter advocates and some researchers, who suggested its methodology was flawed and the results misleading. The 2003 NAEP data were the subject of multiple re-evaluations, including a federal analysis issued in 2006 finding that scores in charter schools, taking into account a

'Green' Charters Forge a Network

At a tiny charter school in Portage, Wis., students don't just take a class in environmental studies. The subject is a defining feature of the school.

"Our curriculum is green," said Victoria J. Rydberg, the founder and lead teacher at River Crossing Environmental Charter School. "Everything we do is tied somehow to environmental studies."

A new organization launched last month, the Green Charter Schools Network, aims to help link up such environmentally focused schools and expand their numbers.

Senn R. Brown, the executive director of the network, based in Madison, Wis., said more and more "green" charters are emerging.

"We're seeing these schools mainly being created by parents and by educators, environmentalists, and so forth," said Mr. Brown, the former head of the Wisconsin Charter Schools Association. "This is the public in public education stepping forward."

The flexibility charter schools generally enjoy is helpful to the approach.

"You have more freedom to create a school from scratch that is often freed from many of the state regulations," Mr. Brown said.

range of background characteristics of students and schools, trailed those in regular public schools that year in reading and math.

Adding to the Debate?

Charter schools, which are publicly funded but largely independent, have been the focus of a growing body of studies. Many experts say the overall findings so far are inconclusive, with a blend of positive, neutral, and negative outcomes for charter schools compared with other public schools.

Todd M. Ziebarth, a senior policy analyst at the National Alliance for Public Charter Schools, a Washington research and advocacy group, said his group is keenly aware of NAEP's limitations, but keeps an eye on the results. "They're important to look

---

At River Crossing Charter, a middle school, the 18 students regularly participate in "real-world restoration projects," said Ms. Rydberg, who just penned a book, *Hands On, Feet Wet: The Story of River Crossing Environmental Charter School.*

She sees advantages to the school's charter status.

"I have to make sure kids meet standards, pass the tests," Ms. Rydberg said. "Other than that, I don't have to go with the district curriculum. It allows me to be very innovative in what we're learning."

Oliver D. Barton, a member of the national network's board and the director of Common Grounds High School in New Haven, Conn., said his school's environmental emphasis is "very helpful in building students' commitment to their own education."

A 1,500-acre park nearby is a field laboratory for learning. The school also runs a small organic farm, growing food for the lunch program.

"You name it: potatoes, squash, beans, chard, lettuces, tomatoes, and eggplants," Mr. Barton said, ticking off produce that reaches the lunchroom. "Pickles are popular."

By Eric Robelen   November 28, 2007

at and learn from, but you learn so little compared to [other] assessments," he said.

Chester E. Finn Jr., the president of the Thomas B. Fordham Foundation, a Washington think tank that is the authorizer for a set of Ohio charter schools, was among the charter advocates who urged the separate reporting of results for charter students on the 2003 NAEP tests. He said he believed it would be good for charter schools and policymakers.

"I hoped they also would be good for traditional public schools, and might show them up," he said.

Mr. Finn said he now believes the most important distinctions are between different kinds of charters, such as those that operate in networks, or from state to state where different governing laws apply.

"I'm not very interested in the average performance of charters," he said. "The word 'charter' signals so little about them, and the diversity within that universe is at least as great as the diversity outside it."

The Charter Sample

The NAEP sample of charter students is designed to be nationally representative, but is dwarfed by the number of students tested in regular public schools.

Recent samples have ranged from 2,300 to 3,300 charter students for each grade level in reading, and from 150 to more than 200 schools. By contrast, in 2007, the national public school sample in 4th grade reading included 183,400 students from 7,310 schools, with somewhat lower 8th grade figures.

The population that charter schools typically serve is substantially different from that served by public schools as a whole, complicating comparisons across school types. In 2007, the NAEP charter sample had more than twice as many black students on a percentage basis and far more students living in cities—groups that generally score below national averages—than did the pool of NAEP test-takers overall.

And the charter population itself is changing, the test samples suggest. For example, 53 percent of charter students tested in 4th grade math in 2007 were eligible for free or reduced-price lunches, up from 42 percent in 2003.

With three rounds of reading and math scores for 4th grade charter students, the NAEP results have not shown clear trends. In reading, charter students' scores apparently rose in 2005 but dropped slightly in 2007; the changes were not large enough, however, to be statistically significant. With 4th graders in regular public schools posting reading gains in 2007, the charter students slipped behind them.

In 4th grade math, charter students have shown what appear to be steady gains from 2003 to 2007—again, not statistically significant—but made little headway in closing the gap with students in regular public schools, who saw a similar growth trend.

Looking at students by race and income status, as measured by eligibility for free or reduced-price lunches, seems to alter the picture.

In 4th grade math, charter students overall were 5 points behind noncharter students in both 2005 and 2007 on the 500-point scale, statistically significant differences.

But for low-income black students, the difference between those in charter schools and those in regular public schools was 1 point in 2005 and 2 points in 2007, neither of which was statistically significant. Measured another way, 56 percent of low-income black students from charter schools scored at the basic level or above in 2007, compared with 59 percent of such students in regular public schools.

"Certainly, the raw data suggest charter students are behind," said Sarah Theule Lubienski, an associate professor of education at the University of Illinois at Urbana-Champaign, after reviewing the recent results for 4th grade students in math and reading. But she said that when controlling for race and low-income status, it appears that "neither one is ahead."

In a press release last September, the national charter alliance highlighted the gains of 8th grade charter students in 2007, though those apparent increases were not deemed statistically significant. The average scale score rose from 255 in 2005 to 260 in 2007 in reading, and from 268 to 273 in math.

Growth Rates Differ?

The alliance concluded that charter students' achievement "increased at a notably faster rate" than that of their peers in regular public schools. It also noted stronger 8th grade gains in certain categories, such as the reading scores for African-American and low-income students.

The charter alliance also noted the performance of Hispanic charter students. In 8th grade math, their average score was 9 points higher than for Hispanics in regular public schools in 2005, and 8 points higher in 2007. Because of the limited charter sample size, though, the differences were not deemed statistically significant.

For its part, the AFT has been quiet about the recent NAEP data. Asked about the results, union spokesman Dan Murphy said, "Basically, what the NAEP data suggests is what we already know. There are some excellent charter schools and some charter schools that fall short. . . . And the same goes for regular public schools."

. . .

GAINS FOR A NEW ORLEANS CHARTER SCHOOL

BY LESLI A. MAXWELL
May 21, 2008

NEW ORLEANS. Most days at the Sophie B. Wright Institute of Academic Excellence, a charter school for 4th through 8th graders in Uptown New Orleans, students encounter someone from a university.

Tutors from Tulane University visit daily. Professors from Southern University at New Orleans arrive to guest teach in a science class. And Alpha Phi Alpha fraternity members from SUNO come most days to mentor boys after school.

Such regular exposure to people connected to higher education, says Principal Sharon Clark, is a key piece of the school's academic model. Those ties have imbued Wright since it was chartered by SUNO in July 2005, the month before Hurricane Katrina devastated the city. Wright, which had been one of New Orleans' most troubled middle schools before the storm, is now producing some of city's most impressive growth in academic achievement. Earlier this month, the school—where nearly all students qualify for free or reduced-price meals—learned that every one of its 4th graders had passed Louisiana's high-stakes exam.

"We know that we can help any child," Ms. Clark said in an interview before learning about the test results. "We've got an intense focus on our academics, and every child in this building can tell you how well they read, and every staff member here knows where their students are doing well and where they are struggling."

The school had been running in its new charter form for only a week when Katrina struck on August 29, 2005. A few months earlier, Wright had been on the verge of being phased out under a districtwide plan in New Orleans to do away with middle schools. But Ms. Clark, who'd managed to raise Wright's dismal test scores modestly since she was hired as principal in 2001, was approached by leaders from SUNO who were interested in chartering a middle school in the city.

"There were so many failing schools in the city, and we felt obligated to get involved and to help turn one around," said Rose Duhon-Sells, the vice chancellor of academic affairs at the university, who also chairs the board that oversees the Sophie B. Wright Institute.

The school became one of five charters approved for New Orleans before the hurricane. And, said Ms. Duhon-Sells, Sophie B. Wright became the nation's first school to be chartered by a historically black institution.

Experienced Teachers

Right away, the newly chartered school became a place where parents would have to be involved on some level. At the very least, they had to come to the school every quarter to pick up their children's report cards. The Success for All program, which uses a schoolwide approach to improve reading skills, was adopted at Wright. And SUNO faculty members were enlisted to help with professional development and to mentor teachers in their disciplines.

But Wright was also striking for what didn't change after it became a charter: Ms. Clark remained as principal. Half the teachers stayed. The students—most of them poor and African-American—were the same.

When Wright reopened after the storm, in January 2006, the school looked different, though. Ms. Clark was back, and many of the teachers returned. But nearly 70 percent of the students hadn't attended Wright before the storm, although like the school's pre-hurricane enrollment, they were mostly black and low-income.

"It was really a matter of which families were able to get back to the city that soon after the storm, and a matter of us being one of the first public schools to reopen," Ms. Clark said. "Many of these kids had experienced the worst of Katrina. They were left on the freeway overpasses, and they were inside the Superdome."

Now, nearly three years after it became a charter and survived Katrina, Wright is thriving.

The 4th grade results on the Louisiana Educational Assessment Program, or LEAP, had the school celebrating this month. In the 8th grade, 62 percent of the students passed LEAP, a 21 percent gain over last year, Ms. Clark said. Fourth and 8th graders who do not pass the exam cannot advance to the next grade.

Wright's scores have improved vastly from the 2004–05 school year, when, as a regular Orleans Parish public school, nearly 83 percent of its 8th graders scored either "approaching basic" or "unsatisfactory" in English language arts, and 76 percent scored in one of those two categories in mathematics. To pass LEAP, students must score at least "basic" in either English or math, and "approaching basic" in the other subject.

Ms. Clark attributes the improvement to several factors. One, she said, is experienced teachers working in classrooms with no more than 20 students. This school year, only one member of Wright's faculty is a first-year teacher. Unlike leaders of other charters in New Orleans and all the schools in the city's state-run Recovery School District, she has not tapped into the Teach For America or Teach NOLA recruitment pool.

"I don't really believe in being a training ground, when these kids need so much," Ms. Clark said.

Charter status—meaning the school is publicly funded but largely independent—has given Ms. Clark a freer hand that goes beyond selecting her staff. She is using single-gender classes in the upper grades for English and math, a strategy that helps "do away with all the nonsense and allows the students to really focus," she said. Ms. Clark brought back Success for All, a reading program she had used at Wright before a New Orleans superintendent decided to get rid of it.

"I don't have to go and ask anyone to do something," Ms. Clark said. "If it works for us, we do it."

Male Mentors

Southern University at New Orleans has a multifaceted role at Sophie B. Wright. The university handles operational tasks such as payroll and other human-resources matters for the school. Ms. Duhon-Sells, who previously served as the dean of the education school at SUNO, visits Wright regularly to observe classroom instruction and to talk with Ms. Clark. SUNO leaders have pledged a scholarship to attend the public university to every Wright 8th grader who graduates from high school.

"I think universities are useless if we don't reach out to these schools and these students early on to connect them to higher education and to demonstrate what is possible," Ms. Duhon-Sells said.

To Wright's male students, it's the Alpha Phi Alpha fraternity members from SUNO who are likely to be making the most lasting impression.

Morkeith Phillips, a 27-year-old senior at SUNO, comes to Wright three days a week to mentor six boys. He studies with the boys, helps them with homework, and acts as a big brother who imparts advice about coping with the struggles of growing up poor in the city. One day earlier this month, he oversaw four boys who were rehearsing a fast-moving, percussive step-dance routine that they would perform for their classmates and teachers.

"It feels good to do this because I know, for me, how valuable it was to have a role model and mentor," said Mr. Phillips, who grew up in one of New Orleans' toughest housing projects and dropped out of high school at 16. "These young men need something to do to keep them from all the negativity on the streets. They need to see that there's more than that life."

James Watson, a 14-year-old 7th grader, said spending time with his mentor "helps keep me on track with my grades." Earlier this year, he'd thought of quitting the mentorship program—one of the requirements is that the boys maintain C grades, at least—but Mr. Phillips would have none of it.

"He wouldn't let me quit," said James. "He made me believe in myself."

. . .

★ A DEFINING MOMENT FOR CHARTER SCHOOLS? ★

How Networking Best Practices May Revolutionize the Movement, and Reshape Urban Education

COMMENTARY BY RICHARD WHITMIRE
AND ANDREW J. ROTHERHAM
February 13, 2008

MANY WHO BOUGHT early personal computers fired them up, wrote a few paragraphs, played some Tetris, and then asked, What's the big deal?

Then came the Internet.

You might want to think of the charter school movement in a similar way. Since the first charter opened in 1992 in St. Paul,

Minn., they have grown quickly, passing the 4,000-school mark. Now there are some outstanding ones and some lemons, but charter schools overall are not proving to be radically dissimilar to other public schools. So what's the big deal?

Call it the "New York effect."

It started four years ago, when New York City Schools chancellor Joel I. Klein attracted a few of the most successful charter networks (the Knowledge Is Power Program, or KIPP; Achievement First; and Uncommon Schools) with dollar-a-year rent offers. All three accepted, but they did more than that: rather than compete, they engaged in what could be called "coopetition," often holding hands as they expanded in the city.

"Instead of fighting each other for resources, we ended up trying to figure out how we can deepen the pool and work together to make resources available for all to grow," says John King from Uncommon Schools. "Each of us visited each other's schools when we were starting up and learned tremendously important lessons."

The intermingling, which began with shared "lessons learned" and expanded into shared training and more, could yield the "Internet" era of charters, a time when the real impact of the idea manifests itself, as the best schools get even better and the low-performing charters (and low-performing public schools and districts) face increasing pressure to improve or close. Powerful, yes. And also a long way from the early vision of charter schools, championed by many on the left as a way to launch more authentic and mom-and-pop public schools, and by many on the right as a way to introduce the relentless pressure of competition into ossified public school systems.

Consider Jabali Sawicki, the principal of the 4-year-old Excellence Charter School in the Bedford-Stuyvesant section of Brooklyn. Sawicki began his career in charters teaching at Boston's strikingly successful Roxbury Preparatory Charter School. He was tapped by leaders at Uncommon Schools (the Roxbury charter's founders) to run the new Bedford-Stuyvesant school.

Then, he received training from KIPP's widely admired school leadership program.

Now several of the teachers in Sawicki's school are earning their master's degrees from a new program at Hunter College, where the founders of all three charter groups, famous names in the charter movement and proven educators such as David Levin of KIPP and Norman Atkins of Uncommon Schools, serve as instructors. And when Sawicki's students reach high school age, many will attend one of the two new high schools now under design for students from these three charter groups. Quarterbacking the new high schools, expected to open in 2010, is the Robin Hood Foundation, the hedge-fund-fueled financial muscle behind this intermingling experiment.

The significance of the cooperation is seen in Excellence Charter's first test scores. Here is a startup school in a poor neighborhood with an all-minority student population, and it is hitting home runs in math and reading. That often doesn't happen with new schools, and yet it *is* happening, not only with Excellence but with the other startup charter schools being spawned by these groups.

Perhaps the most striking payoff from the cooperation is the two-year master's-degree program at Hunter College, which got off the ground when the charter founders discovered their ideal education school dean in the maverick education school reformer David M. Steiner. Led by Steiner, the Hunter faculty embraced the charter founders and this past summer launched a trial version of a program expected to expand rapidly to include not only teachers from other charter schools, but also hundreds of teachers bound for traditional New York City public schools.

The goal was to teach the strategies that make these schools effective. As Uncommon Schools' Atkins explains, planners wanted to "find the best people to teach content, and model and present the methodologies we use most successfully in our own schools." As a result, a class led by this hybrid team looks nothing like a traditional education class. Here, the teachers and students bore in on the little things that define the tenor of the highly structured school day and intensive instruction that mark all three of these schools.

KIPP's co-founder Levin says the goal is to have the expanded Hunter College program replicated in education schools across the country. "This is not about the success of one organization," he says. "It's about sharing what works for kids."

That's a critical goal, but one that in the past has proven elusive in education, where isolated success rather than systemic improvement is the norm. Meanwhile, the challenges facing these elite schools and their leaders remain as substantial as the opportunity they have to reshape urban education.

For starters, all these initiatives remain heavily dependent on philanthropic dollars. Right now, a core group of funders is committed to the ventures, helping them leverage public spending. But philanthropic priorities can change, so the new elites must build durable avenues of support within the public sector.

In addition, although they have grown rapidly, all of the high-performing networks still face the challenge of achieving quality at larger scale. Traditionally, quality and scale in education have been inversely related: as initiatives get larger, fidelity to the elements that made them effective in the first place is compromised. Yet it's not an iron rule. Teach For America, for instance, bucked this trend by growing and maintaining (if not improving) its effectiveness and supplying hundreds of teachers and leaders for the elite networks. KIPP, the largest of these, has expanded and maintained high quality as well. But despite deliberate attention to the key elements of quality, as the networks try to move from impacting thousands of students to millions, the quality-scale challenge will be a test.

The strategy of addressing human capital internally, rather than expecting traditional avenues for teacher and school leadership preparation to do the job, will help. It's also a model that can be replicated elsewhere by reform-oriented superintendents or other networks of high-performing charter schools. And if the elites can help close the gap between teacher preparation and effective practice, that will move the field forward. But David Steiners are in short supply, and it seems unlikely that teacher preparation will dramatically change without a fight.

And, as it often does in education, race is apt to play a role, too. The leadership of many elite initiatives does not look like the students being served. So far, the desperation for better schooling options in many communities has papered this over. But as the elite networks create an even bigger footprint on the urban education landscape, some hard conversations about race and class are inevitable. To their credit, the elites are trying to broaden the pipeline of diverse talent for leadership roles. Still, despite their efforts, an uncomfortable reality lurks just below the surface today.

As the elite networks create an even bigger footprint on the urban education landscape, some hard conversations about race and class are inevitable.

Finally, and most importantly, these initiatives must show that they, and by extension charter schooling, can substantially move the needle on student achievement overall. As Matt Candler, the chief executive officer of New Schools for New Orleans, has remarked, no one wants to be part of a movement whose claim to legitimacy is that it "sucks less" than the other schooling options out there. But if they can get it right, the elites have the potential not just to substantially change the facts on the ground about urban education, but also to earn standing to set the standard for quality overall within public education.

That's a long way from what was launched in Minnesota in 1992, and it could revolutionize American public education.

. . .

★ FEDERAL EDUCATION ★
INNOVATION — GETTING IT RIGHT

COMMENTARY BY TED MITCHELL
AND JONATHAN SCHORR
October 29, 2008

WHEN THE BUSH ADMINISTRATION set out six years ago to create an office of education innovation, it did not envision spending millions of dollars on a museum dedicated to highlighting the importance of New Bedford, Mass., in the 19th-century whaling industry.

As they tout educational innovation on the campaign trail, Sens. Barack Obama and John McCain should take sharp note of how a "nimble, entrepreneurial arm of the U.S. Department of Education" ended up spending hundreds of millions of dollars on not-so-cutting-edge ideas, ranging from the Old Dartmouth Historical Society's whaling museum to a program promoting "the teaching of traditional American history." Reaching agreement on the importance of a muscular federal role in driving education innovation is easier than avoiding the mistakes that have sunk such efforts in the past. If the next president aims to do innovation smarter, there are key steps he must take.

If the next president aims to do innovation
smarter, there are key steps he must take.

Both McCain and Obama have espoused the increasingly widespread view that entrepreneurial organizations, working outside government but in partnership with it, can bring life to new ideas that will get results. In a major education address in Ohio last month, Obama called for a massive expansion of funding for innovative and entrepreneurial efforts, and for more and better charter schools. He cited America's slipping economic competitiveness and called for "a new vision for a 21st-century education—one where we aren't just supporting existing schools, but spurring innovation."

McCain, likewise, has offered support for an entrepreneurial change agenda, going so far as to name pioneering organizations such as Teach For America and the New Teacher Project as allies in his reform effort, and praising reforms favored by many leading innovators, such as rewarding teachers for the performance of their students. Both presidential candidates have been vocal in their support of charter schools, perhaps the leading entrepreneurial strategy for change in education.

It is a wonderful thing that both candidates have made clear their commitment to new forms of public-private partnership. These ideas already are bearing fruit in groups such as the Knowledge Is Power Program, the SEED Foundation, and Aspire Public Schools—organizations that have changed the lives of thousands of low-income children. Bold, smart support for the creation and growth of results-oriented organizations like these will pay handsome dividends for children. Moreover, a major federal investment could dramatically increase the number of powerful new ideas in education, and could help scale up proven entrepreneurial ideas far beyond what private philanthropy can do today—especially given the current financial crisis.

But the long-troubled relationship between the federal government and educational innovation teaches us that the president who takes office in January will need to make some savvy moves to avoid the mistakes of the past. Too often, the forces of bureaucracy and politics have stood in the way of smart investments in innovation, as funding has been diverted to worthwhile but established ideas that do little to change the field. Or, worse, money has been squandered on projects that have done much for their political sponsors, but little for educational progress. From the Nixon-era National Institute of Education—an entity that resembled the National Institutes of Health in name only—to the current Office of Innovation and Improvement, too much federal innovation money has gone the way of the whaling museum.

This is hardly surprising. Indeed, to succeed, a federal innovation office must do exactly what government bureaucracies rarely do well: direct public funds toward unproven ideas, take risks, sustain investments over time, and avoid patronage. To navigate this minefield, the next president must create an education innovation office worthy of the name. It must enjoy enough independence to avoid political pressure and to make risky investments, but sit close enough to the federal education bureaucracy to infect it with an entrepreneurial mind-set, and it must be transparent enough to be a good steward of public money.

In their excellent new paper on education innovation for the Brookings Institution, Andrew J. Rotherham and Sara Mead offer a solution. Noting that private-sector firms often wall off research-and-development departments from the rest of their bureaucracy, Rotherham and Mead argue that the innovation office should be overseen by an independent review board appointed by members of Congress, and headed by an assistant secretary of education. Such a structure would give it influence, visibility, and protection.

Under this structure, a newly minted federal "office of educational entrepreneurship and innovation" would oversee two funds: an Education Innovation Challenge program that would help new ideas with great potential get off the ground, and a Grow What Works program to scale up proven entrepreneurial efforts. Those funds would support the creation and growth of high-performing schools, as well as new strategies for preparing teachers and principals and new tools such as curriculum, assessments, and technology that make schools stronger. Both of the funds would be highly results-oriented, requiring solid evidence that the innovations were leading to meaningful improvement in student performance, and both would be subjected to rigorous evaluation.

Working together, these two programs would stimulate the kind of groundbreaking work in education that the National Institutes of Health do in medicine and the Defense Advanced Research Projects Agency does in the military. Moreover, the availability of such funding would allow leaders of innovative organizations to focus more on work that directly benefits children, rather than the fundraising that consumes so much of their time now. Given the benefit that entrepreneurial ventures such as KIPP and TFA already have provided to low-income children, the value of expanding such efforts, wisely but boldly, would be vast—and could be accomplished at a fraction of what the government spends on military and medical R&D. (It could also be done under existing budget constraints—welcome news amid the current financial woes.)

Yet beyond the two funds, entrepreneurial thinking must function not as an isolated program in the next president's Education Department, but as a mind-set. A nimble, urgent, results-oriented approach cannot be relegated to a single office; it must be the approach that guides the entire department. It's up to the next president to make sure that happens.

Great entrepreneurs harness the pragmatic American spirit to spread what works and redesign what doesn't. In figuring out how to redesign the federal approach to education innovation, the next president must do both.

CHAPTER 4

Make Math and Science National Priorities

"I do not accept an America where elementary school kids are only getting an average of twenty-five minutes of science each day when we know that over 80% of the fastest-growing jobs require a knowledge base in math and science."

BARACK OBAMA

Manchester, N.H., November 20, 2007

THE ISSUE

Fifty years after Sputnik, science and math education is in a crisis in all American schools. For example, in 2003, the Program in International Student Assessment found that U.S. 15-year-olds ranked 28th out of 40 countries in mathematics and 19th out of 40 countries in science.

In the 21st century, everyone needs to know science and math, not only to find employment, but also to be healthy and well-informed citizens. Moreover, over 80 percent of the fastest-growing occupations are dependent upon a knowledge base in science and math.

THE OBAMA PLAN

Obama will make math and science education a national priority, so that we can provide our students with the knowledge and skills they need for the 21st century.

- **Recruit High-Quality Math and Science Teachers:** Prioritize recruiting math, science, and technology degree graduates.

- **Support the Professional Development of Math and Science Teachers:** Support efforts to help new and veteran math and science teachers learn from professionals in the field.

- **Enhance Science Instruction:** Ensure that all children have access to strong science curriculum at all grade levels.

. . .

U.S. STUDENTS LAG BEHIND IN MATH AND SCIENCE

BY KATHLEEN KENNEDY MANZO
December 9, 2008

AMERICAN 4th and 8th graders continue to exceed the international average on math and science tests, but are still well behind their counterparts in several Asian nations and trail a few European countries, results released today show.

Students in Massachusetts and Minnesota who took part in the testing program, however, excelled ahead of their peers across the United States. Massachusetts in particular did as well as some of the leading Asian nations in some areas.

The Third International Mathematics and Science Study, or TIMSS, an ongoing assessment program sponsored by the International Association for the Evaluation of Educational Achievement, is sure to fuel the discussion about the adequacy of the effort in U.S. schools to improve instruction and curricula in the subjects.

"It's a good-news, bad-news kind of story. In mathematics, the U.S. is making steady progress, and since 1999, has significantly improved," said Ina V.S. Mullis, an executive director of the TIMSS

& PIRLS International Study Center at Boston College, part of the international association. "However, the gap between the U.S. and top-performing Asian countries is huge, just enormous."

'Relative Position'

Gains in math among U.S. students over more than a decade parallel efforts to improve instruction in the subject, a focus that has not been evident in science education, according to Stuart Kerachsky, the acting commissioner of the National Center for Education Statistics, a branch of the U.S. Department of Education.

"We've kept our relative position to Asian countries, which have been the high fliers," he said. "We see basically continued strong performance, but nothing that changes where the U.S. stands [internationally]."

While school reform efforts have increasingly focused on improving instruction and teacher training in math and science, some experts say those efforts are wholly inadequate.

"For the last 10 years, we've seen many reports that say we need to be investing more in science education, yet very little filtered down into the classroom," said Francis Q. Eberle, the executive director of the National Science Teachers Association, based in Arlington, Va. "What's important about TIMSS is that we can learn how we're doing as a country relative to other countries, and where we need to be focusing on. So until this country decides that science is important, results like this shouldn't be surprising."

Among the most promising of the results for the United States, 4th graders improved significantly on the math assessment since it was last given in 2003. They scored 529 points on a 1,000-point scale, a jump of 11 points. That group scored 539 points on the science test, statistically the same as several years ago. Eighth graders gained a few points over the previous test, to score 508, but the gain was not statistically significant. Since 1995, however, 8th graders have gained 16 points, a significant increase, according to the report.

In science, American 8th graders scored 520 points, a drop since 2003 that was not considered significant.

Singapore, China's special administrative region of Hong Kong, and Taiwan dominated on the 4th grade tests. They were joined by South Korea and Japan as leaders among the 8th graders. Several developing Eastern European countries—the Czech Republic, Hungary, Latvia, Russia, and Slovenia—outscored the United States in some areas.

Exceeding the Average

Both 4th graders and 8th graders in the United States significantly exceeded the international average in the percentages of students who met "intermediate," "high," and "advanced" benchmarks in both subjects. But much larger percentages of students in top-performing countries demonstrated advanced understanding of the subjects. On the math test, for example, at least 40 percent of 4th and 8th graders in Singapore and Hong Kong, and the same percent of 8th graders in Taiwan and South Korea, scored at the advanced level.

The State of Science in America

Three-quarters of adults say they do not have a good understanding of science, and 80 percent say the subject should receive more attention in schools, a survey commissioned by the Museum of Science and Industry in Chicago has found.

A majority of adults questioned, 70 percent, said the United States is not a world leader in science, and about the same percentage said the country would not be a world leader in science within the next 20 years, largely because of a lack of funding and high-quality instruction in science education.

Data for the report were gathered by Harris Interactive, a Rochester, N.Y.-based company that conducts opinion polls. The nationally representative telephone survey, taken in November and December of 2007, polled 1,300 adults.

By Mary C. Breaden   March 26, 2008

The TIMSS assessments seek to measure students' mastery of specific content they have learned in science and math classes, as well as cognitive dimensions, such as knowing, applying, and reasoning. The study contrasts with the goal of a separate international comparison released late last year, the Program for International Student Assessment, or PISA, which gauges 15-year-olds' abilities at applying math skills to real-world contexts. U.S. students tend to perform better on TIMSS than on PISA.

But direct comparisons are potentially problematic, Mr. Kerachsky said, when observers consider the size and diversity of the United States when compared with some of the leaders.

"Turning things around and changing a country that has the diversity of the U.S. is difficult," he said. Comparing American students with a representative sampling of children in China, as opposed to Taiwan, would likely yield a much different result, he added.

On the 2007 assessment, 425,000 students from 59 countries participated. Eight other "benchmarking" sites, including regional entities in Canada, Dubai in the United Arab Emirates, and the U.S. states of Massachusetts and Minnesota, took part and received results that can be compared with their countries' data and be used to gauge their achievement on international benchmarks.

Samples of students in Massachusetts and Minnesota who took the tests provided perhaps the best news for the United States. Massachusetts' 4th graders, for example, scored 571 points on the science test, a score that was outdone only by Singapore, which scored 587. In math, 4th graders from the Bay State scored 572, with Hong Kong, Singapore, and Taiwan doing better. At the 8th grade level, only the top-performing Asian countries did better than Massachusetts in either subject.

Minnesota also did significantly better than the United States overall, and outscored the likes of Japan on the 4th grade science test. The state, however, fell behind the other top Asian nations on all the tests.

The success of those two states, some experts say, demonstrates how setting rigorous standards and putting resources into aligning the curriculum and professional development to those standards can lead to improved student achievement.

"Here you have two states that have clear, focused, rigorous math standards and sustained attention to improving teaching and learning, and as a result, Massachusetts is scoring very high and Minnesota at the 4th grade level showed phenomenal gains," said Michael Cohen, the president of Achieve, the Washington-based organization that is studying the academic standards of high-performing countries. "For those who say we can't compete with some other countries, this calls that into question."

The gains for Minnesota are particularly impressive, some experts say, when you consider the state did not have standards when the first TIMSS was given in 1995. The state later decided to use the lessons learned from the curriculum studies of TIMSS to create standards that reflect some of the features of the top nations in the world, said William H. Schmidt, the Michigan State University researcher who conducted those studies.

"Minnesota moved from mediocrity to a reasonably elite status. They're right up there, just underneath the top-tier countries," he said. "This says, yes, you can do this, and here's the way can do this."

Innovation Counts

Critics of such comparisons, though, have argued that the international test results do not predict a country's success. Gerald Bracey, a Port Townsend, Wash.-based researcher and author, said that despite the test scores, the United States is ranked atop all nations on indices of global competitiveness, and American workers are deemed the most productive in the world. And the tests don't necessarily measure such qualities as creativity, ambition, and innovation, for which the United States is noted, he added.

"It has been pointed out that Singapore students fade once they hit the real world," Mr. Bracey said. "Innovation is the one aspect of economic competitiveness that does not at some point show diminishing returns. Bigger or faster airplanes can only improve productivity so much. Innovation has no limits."

For the first time, the TIMSS report includes an extensive online encyclopedia that details a number of categories for each country.

"The encyclopedia tries to provide as full a picture as possible of the culture, the curriculum, the goals, and aims of [a nation's] schools," said Michael O. Martin, who directs the international-study center with Ms. Mullis. "So you have all that information that is hard to quantify," he said, but that helps put the data in context.

·   ·   ·

SCIENTISTS NURTURE TEACHERS' GROWTH

BY SEAN CAVANAGH
November 28, 2007

IMAGINE A CLASSROOM filled with thousands of feet of cable and a pair of microscopes four stories high. Students work alongside top-tier scientists, who use the surrounding instruments to probe nuclear matter in the hope of one day producing breakthroughs in science and technology.

The classroom in this case is known as Hall A, located in the Thomas Jefferson National Accelerator Facility. And the students are science teachers, who come to the federal laboratory in Newport News, Va., as part of an unusual professional-development opportunity.

The Academies Creating Teacher Scientists program pairs top federal scientists from the U.S. Department of Energy with middle and high school teachers from around the country who want to improve their classroom skills.

Teachers spend four to eight weeks for three consecutive summers under the tutelage of scientists at federal labs of their choice, crafting activities and lessons they can use in their classrooms.

The program is just one of many sponsored by federal agencies that offer training to mathematics and science teachers. Although some officials question the effectiveness of those efforts, they have proved popular with teachers seeking help beyond what they can find on the more traditional circuit of educator workshops and conferences.

One first-year participant in the Energy Department's program this past summer was Joseph J. Amma, an 8th grade teacher from North East Middle School, in Maryland, about 50 miles from Baltimore. Mr. Amma was one of 17 science teachers who were introduced to scientific equipment and resources at the lab, then worked together with help from federal scientists to design simple in-class activities and experiments based on the science they saw there.

"We didn't have someone just talking at us," Mr. Amma said. "We were physically engaged, rather than someone just coming in and giving us a lecture." The scientists at the lab, he said, showed the teachers "very simple concepts, taken to a very advanced level."

A Confidence Game

About 200 teachers have taken part so far in the academies program, which was launched in 2004 and has a $2.3 million annual budget. Educators apply online to work at any of 12 Energy Department labs across the country with researchers who specialize in a variety of fields, not just energy.

Participating teachers work with mentor-scientists, who guide them through research projects and provide them with seminars and demonstrations related to the lab's work. Teachers also draw up online professional-development plans describing how they will continue to improve their teaching skills, and they write curricula based on lab experiences. They are encouraged to stay in touch with the lab scientists during the school year.

Teachers receive stipends of $800 a week during the program, and can apply for grants of up to $4,000 per year to buy lab equipment for their classes and to pursue other professional development. Depending on how far their homes are from the federal energy facilities, they can live in housing at the labs. Mr. Amma, whose school is located in North East, Md., and another teacher from there, Jennifer L. Everett—who also happens to be his fiancée—took that option, bunking in the same facility as visiting scientists and students who come from around the world to work at the Jefferson accelerator facility.

Expert Tutors

Teachers accepted to the Academies Creating Teacher Scientists program spend four to eight weeks picking up classroom ideas and skills from scientists.

Program Features:

Size: About 200 teachers have participated so far.

Support: In addition to on-site training, teachers receive stipends and can apply for grant funding for classroom materials, further training, and travel.

Locations: 12 U.S. Department of Energy labs train teachers through the program:

- Ames National Laboratory (Iowa)
- Argonne National Laboratory (Ill.)
- Brookhaven National Laboratory (N.Y.)
- Fermi National Accelerator Laboratory (Ill.)
- Idaho National Laboratory (Idaho)
- Lawrence Berkeley National Laboratory (Calif.)
- Lawrence Livermore National Laboratory (Calif.)
- National Renewable Energy Laboratory (Colo.)
- Oak Ridge National Laboratory (Tenn.)
- Pacific Northwest National Laboratory (Wash.)
- Sandia National Laboratories (N.M.)
- Thomas Jefferson National Accelerator Facility (Va.)

Source: U.S. Department of Energy

A typical day, Ms. Everett said, began with a lecture from a lab scientist, followed by a presentation or tour of one part of the facility. Afternoons were spent on group activities focused on improving classroom skills. Teachers also built equipment for their classes from scratch, based on the science under discussion. They were expected to reflect on their observations in online journals.

The goal, as with many professional-development programs, is to produce teachers skilled and confident enough to act as leaders who can help their colleagues when they return to their home districts, said Jan Tyler, the science education manager at the Jefferson lab.

Building that confidence takes time. It's easy for teachers to feel intimidated by their mentors, who have vast scientific knowledge and lengthy professional credentials, Ms. Tyler noted. The Jefferson lab, which has a total staff of about 700 employees, conducts cutting-edge research on nuclear physics, with a focus on the nucleus of the atom.

"The teachers feel like they're not as important as the scientists are. That's something we're trying to fix," Ms. Tyler said. "They need to hear that they're very important to the future of this country. They don't hear that enough."

Douglas W. Higinbotham, a staff scientist who has worked with teachers in the program, appreciates the role educators play. He remembers how two of his high school teachers—in junior-year chemistry and senior-year physics—helped set him on his professional path.

"They were not big on memorization—they were big on concepts," he said. "That really got me hooked."

Mr. Higinbotham, a nuclear physicist, tries to follow a similar philosophy in working with teachers. He introduces them to various concepts and discusses how lab instruments are used, such as the massive microscopes in Hall A known as spectrometers.

One of his recent projects centered on cosmic rays—particles that flood Earth from beyond its atmosphere, though they cannot be seen or felt. He had teachers research the topic on their own, and, over the course of several weeks, introduced them to the techniques scientists use to detect the rays. He wants teachers not only to understand the concept, but also how scientists study phenomena that are not readily detectable.

Along with the Department of Energy, federal agencies overseeing training programs for math and science teachers include the U.S. Department of Education, the National Science Foundation, and the National Aeronautic and Space Administration.

NASA has long been involved in K–12 education. The agency stages institutes for 300 to 500 teachers preparing to enter classrooms and offers programs that serve about 1,000 current science and mathematics educators a year, said Jim Stofan, a deputy assistant administrator for the space agency.

Addressing Weaknesses

Those federal programs have come under increasing pressure to show results, however. A report released in May questioned the effectiveness of 105 math and science programs with combined budgets of $3 billion scattered across agencies, including those focused on teachers. Congress mandated the report, which was released by the Academic Competitiveness Council, a federal panel chaired by U.S. Secretary of Education Margaret Spellings.

The Energy Department has established a process for evaluating the academies that is consistent with the council's report and will take effect in fiscal 2008, said Bill Valdez, the agency's associate director of workforce development for teachers and scientists.

But he also noted that department officials initially designed the academies based on what he regards as research-proven strategies—namely, giving teachers sustained support, rather than one-time help, and connecting them with mentor scientists and exceptional teachers. "We were pretty confident going into the program that it would be successful," Mr. Valdez said in an e-mail.

For Mr. Amma and Ms. Everett, the Maryland teachers, the chance to study at a federal lab, and bring that experience back to their classrooms, was too good to pass up.

Among the most productive activities, Ms. Everett said, were sessions in which she and other teachers were asked to examine their strengths and weaknesses in the classroom—and come up with activities to help them address their shortcomings. She wanted ideas about devising activities that could be used with both high- and low-performing science students. Over the summer, with help from other teachers and the lab's staff members, Ms. Everett conceived projects that focused on eddy currents and electrical fields, which she will use with both groups.

Lab officials broadened teachers' knowledge of science by asking them to build various devices from scratch. Ms. Everett and Mr. Amma were both asked to construct a "ring fling," a small, pole-like object made of wire, pipe, and other materials, which the teachers plan to use this school year in their lessons on electricity and magnetism.

Mr. Amma has produced a slide show of his experiences at the lab, which demonstrates various high-tech equipment at work. It's been a hit, so he's trying to space the show out over the semester to keep students hooked.

"I thought they would get sick of them, but the kids keep wanting [more]," said Mr. Amma, who remarks that his own enthusiasm has been rekindled. "When you come back, you have genuine excitement for science," he said. "It changes you in what you see scientifically."

.   .   .

LABS AT ELEMENTARY LEVEL
HELP BRING SCIENCE ALIVE

BY SEAN CAVANAGH
June 4, 2008

OLATHE, KAN. How do you judge the power of a simple science experiment? Step inside a 4th grade classroom—and behold the near-total silence.

One recent day, elementary teacher Jamie Curbow achieved just that, as she organized her students into teams for a competition to see who could build the strongest possible miniature bridge, using plastic straws, tape, and scissors to span the distance between lab tables.

Ms. Curbow moved from bridge to bridge, testing the strength of each one in turn. She tied a tin can to a string and hung it from each bridge's center. Then, she began slowly loading the can with golf balls.

The first bridge held three balls, the second one, nine. The higher the count, the quieter the children got.

The teacher at Prairie Creek Elementary School, just southwest of Kansas City, captivated her elementary pupils through a core science-class activity—an easy experiment—that educators and advocates say is vital to building enthusiasm and understanding for the subject in the early grades.

State and district science standards typically call for students to take part in hands-on labs and experiments in the elementary grades. The 1996 National Science Education Standards, which were written by the National Research Council and serve as a reference for many states, emphasize similar activities.

Yet the use of even simple labs and experiments in early grades varies widely, say many observers, largely because of the pressure to devote time to other subjects, but also because elementary teachers lack experience and confidence in setting up those lessons.

Teachers here at Prairie Creek and other elementary schools in Kansas' 1,900-student Spring Hill district are trying to give science labs and in-class experiments more weight. The district, with the financial assistance of a grant, is carving out more time for those hands-on lessons and using science "coaches" who meet regularly with teachers like Ms. Curbow to help them craft those activities. The elementary school even sets aside a room—a lab—specifically for science.

In the bridge project, Ms. Curbow, with help from Linda Sullivan, the district science coach, is teaching a basic lesson on the scientific process, from conducting research to running an experiment, and examining the results to see what did or did not work. And her charges are taking it very seriously.

After testing several bridges, Ms. Curbow kneels beside Group Five's creation and begins adding golf balls to the tin can.

The record now stands at 13 balls, but Group Five is making a big push.

"Ten. Eleven. Twelve," Ms. Curbow says, pausing after each new ball to see if the bridge holds.

Boys and girls silently mouth the count with her, or whisper to each other. Some squeeze below the two tables, as the bridge begins to buckle and sag.

The count reaches 14—and the bridge stands. The students erupt in cheers for the new record holder. Finally, at the 15th ball, the structure collapses with a clatter.

Science Comeback?

Before beginning the experiment, Ms. Curbow reviewed different bridge designs the students had discussed in class, such as arch, beam, and suspension models. Now, she asks the class to review the experiment. What were the features of the bridges that held up the longest, she asks?

Their straws were bunched together, one student says. Metallic scissors were used as anchors, another adds.

And the weakest bridges? "One of them was way too spread out," a boy tells the teacher, "one straw here, one straw there."

Unlike students in many elementary schools, Ms. Curbow's 4th graders are conducting science in a room reserved solely for that subject. A sign on the door says "Welcome Scientists." Photos of students doing science decorate the walls. The room includes eight long lab tables, more common in high schools than in those serving early grades. It is available throughout the day, and students are encouraged to come to monitor their investigations, involving earthworms, plants, and other living things, Ms. Sullivan says.

Those efforts would probably hearten scientists and science educators, who have complained in recent years that science has been pushed out of the curriculum, particularly in the early grades. Many blame the federal No Child Left Behind Act, which requires annual testing in reading and mathematics and mandates that schools raise scores in those subjects or face increasingly stiff penalties.

But Linda Froschauer, a former president of the National Science Teachers Association, believes science labs, and science overall, are now gaining ground in elementary schools as a result of more recently implemented mandates in the federal law that apply to science.

During the 2007–08 academic year, states for the first time were required to start testing students annually in science in the 3–5, 6–9, and 10–12 grade spans. Still, schools do not face the same penalties for not raising science scores as they do in math and reading, unless states voluntarily attach such weight to science.

Many of the newly created state tests are attempting to evaluate students' skills in scientific "inquiry"—generally speaking, their ability to acquire knowledge through the activities and processes used by actual scientists, Ms. Froschauer said.

Labs are an obvious way to instill those skills in students of all ages, she said. "You have to participate in science to do that," said Ms. Froschauer, an elementary math and science curriculum leader in the 2,500-student Weston, Conn., school district.

Even without having separate rooms to conduct experiments, many elementary teachers find ways to lead students through basic hands-on activities involving plants and insects in their traditional classrooms, Ms. Froschauer added.

An obvious benefit of elementary-level hands-on activities is their ability to boost children's enthusiasm for science, said Michael Lach, a former science director for the Chicago public school system. But teachers also need to use labs to challenge young students and connect activities to important science content, added Mr. Lach, now the officer for high school teaching and learning in the 409,000-student district.

The challenge is to move from labs that are not only "different, fun, and engaging," Mr. Lach explained, but are also "developing [a specific] kind of scientific idea."

Readying Teachers

A big barrier to conducting effective science labs in elementary schools is finding teachers who are skilled enough to make them work. Ms. Curbow, 27, acknowledges that she was stronger in reading and math than science, when she graduated from college with a degree in elementary education.

But over the past two years, her confidence and skill have grown. Beginning in the 2006–07 school year, she met regularly with Ms. Sullivan, one of three science coaches in the district's three elementary schools, who helped her plan science lessons and led those activities at first. In the academic year now ending, Ms. Curbow took the lead in those in-class activities.

"It's very beneficial," Ms. Curbow said of the coaching. "What's great about this program is, if [teachers] don't know the answer, we admit it."

The Spring Hill district's venture is supported with a three-year, $280,000 grant from the Ewing Marion Kauffman Foundation, based in Kansas City, Mo. The foundation has awarded $15 million in grants to 13 districts across the Kansas City region, all devoted to improving math and science education.

Districts are using that money in a variety of ways, but paying for science coaches and elementary science labs is a common strategy. (The Kauffman Foundation also helps support coverage of science education in *Education Week*.)

Staying on Task

Science labs came more easily for Cindy McGrew than for some elementary teachers. Ms. McGrew, who works at New Central Elementary School in Havana, Ill., used to be a middle school science teacher. For one of her labs, she collects, treats, and germinates prairie seeds, using a small prairie garden maintained by her 500-student school. She tests physical and chemical reactions, using household ammonia, laundry material, and Epsom salts.

Next year, she said, her school will begin using the Full Option

Science System, or FOSS, a Berkeley, Calif.-based curriculum that offers hands-on experiments for elementary students.

Ms. McGrew sympathizes with teachers who worry about their ability to keep youngsters focused—and even safe—during a science lab. She said she tries to seize on students' enthusiasm for experiments to get them to take those lessons seriously.

"I explain that there are two ways to do science," said Ms. McGrew, referring to hands-on activities and reading about science in a textbook. "What do you like best?" she asks them.

"Then let's make sure we do what the teacher says, and stay on task."

.   .   .

A SCHOOL WHERE STEM IS KING

BY ANDREW TROTTER
March 27, 2008

BALTIMORE. A visit to Baltimore Polytechnic Institute creates a strong impression: This is a place for doers.

Teachers and students at Poly, as it is known here, seem to gather up knowledge and information because they have a use for it. A student is doing background research for her two-year project with local scientists on cannibalism among blue crabs. A group of teenagers searches the Web for a design concept to improve a robot they are entering in a contest. And an aeronautics class discusses the afternoon's weather forecast—as measured from the roof of the school—as a factor in flying several radio-controlled model helicopters.

That focus on applied information is a clue to the bigger purpose at this public school on the northern end of the Baltimore school district: To be a caldron for the blending disciplines known as STEM—science, technology, engineering, and mathematics.

STEM "is blending practice with theory," says Barney J. Wilson, the energetic leader of the school. "Folks talk about STEM as if it were in a box, but it's a way of thinking and living. To really understand it, you have to live it."

For the past two decades, the high school—which for more than a century was organized around manual arts and, later, vocational technology—has remolded itself around STEM.

Robert Marinelli, who arrived 14 years ago and is now the head of Poly's science department, helped convert hand-drafting studios and wood, sheet-metal, hot-metal, and machine shops into computer and design labs, an aviation lab, and other modern learning spaces.

Just as important, he and other teachers developed courses that addressed the T and the E in the STEM acronym, starting with a yearlong course on the fundamentals of engineering that every Poly freshman must pass through.

Today, with STEM education on the lips of national and business leaders and a growing cadre of educators, the 1,350-student school finds itself in a position of leadership.

Admissions Criteria

Poly is one of a handful of selective public high schools in Baltimore, with admission based on criteria favoring students with good grades and recommendations by their middle school teachers and counselors.

"We look for students who have shown aptitude in math and a love for science; also, students who are serious about school," as reflected in good attendance in middle school, Wilson says.

The school has plenty of choices of students. For the 2007–08 school year, 1,800 students from across the city applied for 430 freshman spots.

The current enrollment is 78 percent African-American and evenly split between boys and girls. Nearly all its students are aiming for higher education, Wilson says proudly.

He says the school's three secrets to success are a great faculty, a history of success, and great students.

But Poly has other assets to draw upon, such as the fervent loyalty of its large pool of alumni: the school's database has 20,000 individuals, including members of the city's business, higher education, and government establishment. They provide crucial contacts and give money that supplements the formula funding that the 82,000-student Baltimore district provides each of its high schools.

And some graduates have come home to Poly to teach, bringing lessons from the broader world of industry and academia.

STEM at Poly

Wilson, himself a Poly grad, earned undergraduate degrees in electrical engineering, economics, and math at Carnegie Mellon University before completing a master's degree in industrial administration and a doctorate in urban educational leadership.

From Carnegie Mellon, Wilson brought a belief in an interdisciplinary approach to creativity and problem-solving that the university calls the "Da Vinci effect." It means that students should have an education that is interdisciplinary, that uses both sides of the brain, that includes a deep understanding of art "almost to the point of being connoisseurs," and that gives them leadership roles, Wilson says.

The school advertises the concept well. A portrait of Leonardo da Vinci, the quintessential Renaissance man, gazes down from a wall in the school's media lab. Students arriving at the sprawling school as freshmen quickly learn what STEM stands for, and the four letters are splashed across a couple of huge bulletin boards in the corridors.

Other banners trumpet the school's latest scores on the Maryland high school science assessment—a 93.4 percent passing rate on the biology assessment: "Let's be the first to 100 percent," it urges—and publicize the Siemens Competition in Math, Science, & Technology and the Intel Science Talent Search, two of the most prominent national contests in the STEM disciplines.

Glass-covered bulletin boards also recount the triumphs of the school's "Research Superstars"—three top-10 national finishers in the Intel contest over the past three school years—just a few steps from a display of interscholastic sports trophies.

The school's commitment to STEM is also built into the curriculum, starting with a course required for all 9th graders, called Foundations of Technology (Fundamentals of Engineering). The course gets students to consider technology as more than iPods or flat-screen TVs; they study the history of technology and explore its relationship to engineering, as well as to science and math.

"Technology is the application, or the fulfillment, of engineering," explains Michael J. Scott, one of the teachers of the course. "Engineering is the application of math and science and technical principles."

Scott, who goes by "Mick," teaches concepts, practice, and application in nine core areas of technology—such as electrical, electronic, structural, and fluid—or as many areas as he can get to before the year runs out.

His spacious classroom is in a former sheet-metal shop, with the conversion still incomplete, where students work on plywood sheets laid across old metal cabinets—but with airy, high ceilings, natural lighting, and an old maple floor.

The nine personal computers at one end of the room are more than 8 years old, which requires that they use an old edition of Auto-CAD design software; Scott plans to install an Internet connection in the classroom this summer so his students can conveniently use the Web for research rather than having to schedule time in one of the school's computer labs.

But the classroom also has a cluster of band saws and drill presses so students can learn to make working models of technological designs. Scott shows off one model his students designed and constructed—a dialysis machine, made of plywood, plastic tubing, and an assortment of plastic bags. "I was shocked at how well it worked," in separating yellow and red from orange dye, Scott says.

One change of pace that 9th graders enjoy during the technology and engineering course is a two-week stint in Poly's aeronautics lab.

Tucked away in a corner of the school is a collection of 14 flight simulators—desktop computers equipped with authentic flight-steering harnesses, foot pedals, and simulation software.

The lab also has a life-size mock-up of the nose assembly of an aircraft and real runway signs donated by a local airport. It is equipped for model rocketry, radio-controlled model planes and helicopters, and access to real-time meteorological data from the weather station on the school roof.

Though the 9th graders get only a taste of the science of flying, students in Poly's Air Force Junior ROTC program take a full-year flying course, covering the ground training needed to qualify for a pilot's license, says the teacher, Air Force Maj. Roger Gauert.

Getting on Track

Poly gives students chances to explore a wide range of subjects in grades 9 and 10, but by junior year they must select one of two tracks: science or engineering. From that point, the program is highly scripted.

The science track, however, includes the option of a research "practicum," an opportunity to conduct research for up to two years under the mentorship of a professional scientist in the area; students often enter their research projects in high school contests that can give them an edge, and possibly scholarship money, when they apply to colleges.

Both tracks, however, aim to mold students to think scientifically, to put things in perspective, and to solve problems—and to be more than ready for postsecondary studies, Wilson says.

"Our students have a good shot at making a 4.0 in their first year of college," he boasts.

The science track is "pretty much nose to the grindstone," says Lissa R. Rotundo, a science teacher, who teaches courses in genetics and Advanced Placement biology.

Her classroom, a bright, spacious hall next door to Mick Scott's, is another former machine shop that was fully renovated a few years ago with a state grant. It has distinct zones for lecture, reference books, laboratory activities, and Web research on new-looking iMac computers.

But Rotundo, who has taught at Poly for 23 years and wears a beaded necklace shaped like a double-helix strand of DNA, also directs a forensic-science class for 12th graders—an elective class that gives hardworking seniors a respite by requiring no outside homework. But the class is firmly grounded in the STEM philosophy, Rotundo notes, because it pulls together so many disciplines.

"They come in here and say. 'Oh, you really can use that,'" she says of students' reaction. "They take the course because they think it's 'CSI,'" Rotundo says, referring to the popular television drama on crime-scene investigation. But as they learn and practice chromatography, fiber analysis, hair analysis, blood-spatter analysis, and DNA fingerprinting, their knowledge and techniques from chemistry and genetics come into play.

The evident success of Poly, an elite school with talented students, raises the issue of whether "cream skimming," especially in an urban environment, benefits the school district and Baltimore's student population as a whole.

To that question, Marinelli, the science department head, responds that if the resources and students assembled at Poly and the other specialty schools were dispersed among all the city's high schools, some families would vote with their feet and move to suburban Baltimore County or enroll their children in private schools if they could afford it.

"We'd lose something really valuable, and we'd never get it back," he says.

Of Poly students who are juniors this year, 100 percent have passed the state's high school science exam, either their first time or after a dose of remediation, according to school officials.

Real-World Experiences

It is important to Marinelli that people realize that Poly students have authentic experiences in science. "They are active scientists, not science students," he declares, of the science practicum. "People think they're washing glassware."

Yet another technology teacher at Poly, Fred Nastvogel, an architect by training, says today's students are less well equipped to handle the real-world, physical aspects of their studies, compared with students a couple of decades ago.

"Many youngsters don't do chores anymore; they don't learn to repair or build things with their hands. Kids have never had the experience of grabbing stuff and making something happen," Nastvogel says. The lack of such experiences, he adds, limits their understanding of how "things go round and round in the universe" and concepts such as how nanoparticles work.

Essential to what he calls the "primitive STEM experience" that high schools should offer, he says, is giving students plenty of experience working with modeling and materials.

Poly is in the midst of planning an engineering-research practicum that will resemble the science-research practicum, Marinelli says. It would provide coursework in advanced engineering for 11th and 12th graders, plus field experiences with professional engineers.

Such a program would likely spur more student projects in engineering, such as an invention by Poly senior Michelle Jones that is meant to help prevent drivers from falling asleep at the wheel. She has designed a dashboard-mounted video camera that monitors a driver's eyes and triggers an alarm if the blink-rate slows or speeds up significantly.

Innovation, of course, is meant to be one of the main fruits of a rich STEM curriculum, yet that term is not well understood, and often confused with invention, teachers at Poly say.

"Bill Gates invented, but that is a rarity," Marinelli says of the Microsoft co-founder, who developed the world's most widely used computer operating software and office software suite. "Certainly, I'm telling students that most of the technology you are going to use in your lifetime has already been invented. You are going to make it better—you are efficiency experts."

Whatever the label given to the product of focused creativity in STEM, school leaders say Poly students are so well prepared that their success after school is virtually assured. "I could grab any three students here and start a business—and in 10 years we'd be a Fortune 500," Director Wilson says.

Program Aims to Build 'Ingenuity'

It can be a tall order for many schools to help students excel in STEM subjects. But the Baltimore district has gotten a hand from a foundation-led initiative aimed at doing just that.

The $1 million-per-year Ingenuity Project, begun in 1992 and led by the locally based Abell Foundation, supports about 500 selected students in grades 6–12 at two middle schools and a high school. Goals include succeeding on Advanced Placement tests and excelling in elite national competitions in mathematics, science, engineering, technology, and related fields.

Students apply to take part in middle school; all must reapply for 9th grade. Students are grouped together for science and math, but are blended into regular classes for other subjects.

At Baltimore Polytechnic Institute, a STEM-focused high school that draws students from across the city, Ingenuity students in grades 9–12 take part in independent research projects in science lasting two or three school years, including work in the summers.

"They can dig into something, learning things not in a textbook but on the cutting edge," says Dolores Costello, the executive director of the Ingenuity Project.

David Nelson, the research director at Poly, whose position is funded by the project, helps students find their research topics and a Baltimore-area scientist to mentor them at an outside facility.

"We try to give students as much autonomy and responsibility to make their own decision to define their own interests," Nelson says. "It is valuable for the student to go through that process."

CHAPTER 5

Address the Dropout Crisis

"Now is the time to finally meet our moral obligation to provide every child a world-class education, because it will take nothing less to compete in the global economy."

BARACK OBAMA

Denver, August 28, 2008

THE ISSUE

Only 70 percent of U.S. high school students graduate with a diploma. African-American and Latino students are significantly less likely to graduate than white students. Today, dropouts are twice as likely to be unemployed, and for those who work, pay is low, advancement limited, and health insurance less available. Barack Obama and Joe Biden will address dropout by supporting programs that help students in struggling schools before it's too late.

THE OBAMA PLAN

To help our most at-risk children succeed in school, the Obama-Biden plan will:

- **Address the Dropout Crisis:** Obama and Biden will address the dropout crisis by passing legislation to provide funding to school districts to invest in intervention strategies in middle school—strategies such as personal academic plans, teaching teams, parent involvement, mentoring, intensive reading and math instruction, and extended learning time.

- **Support English Language Learners:** Obama and Biden support transitional bilingual education and will help Limited English Proficient students get ahead by holding schools accountable for making sure these students complete school.

. . .

MOTIVATING STUDENTS
IN THE MIDDLE YEARS

BY KATHLEEN KENNEDY MANZO
March 19, 2008

DURHAM, N.C. It's not easy to hide in Amber Cline's math class.

Even the most skilled evaders among the 7th graders at Rogers-Herr Middle School here can't dodge the veteran teacher's questioning and prodding during a lesson on scale factors and ratios.

The earnest teacher has learned just how hard to push to keep her students focused on the illustrated math problems they are working on, and when to ease up if one gets frustrated or seems close to turning her off. She's honed that instinct throughout the school year as she's gotten to know each of her students' academic strengths and weaknesses, as well as their personalities, moods, and quirks.

"For the kids who aren't self-motivated and don't have support at home, we need to stand over them and say get this done," Ms. Cline said. "We know what each kid needs as far as applying pressure or giving support. . . . They know we will not allow them to fail."

Ms. Cline and her colleagues in this school have worked at melding rigorous subject matter with the demands of test-driven accountability, while also attending to the developmental, family, and social issues their 625 predominantly minority and lower-income students face.

More than a decade after a prominent group of middle-grades reformers set out to infuse higher academic standards into what critics deemed the touchy-feely world of middle schools, many teachers are still grappling with ways to motivate students to excel intellectually while helping them adapt to the dramatic physical and emotional changes that come with puberty.

That mix of rigor, relevance, and responsiveness, experts say, is crucial for guiding students, particularly those most at risk of dropping out, on the path to high school graduation and later success. Too many schools serving 6th through 9th graders, however, have yet to find the right prescription for keeping those youngsters engaged at a time when their growing curiosity, independence, and need for the acceptance of their peers may lead them to act out or zone out in school.

Benefits of Early Intervention

"Our belief is they'll grow out of it. But the evidence shows that in high-poverty environments, they don't grow out of it" without intervention, said Robert Balfanz, a research scientist at the Center for the Social Organization of Schools, based at Johns Hopkins University in Baltimore. "As soon as kids are off track, we need to aggressively approach these issues."

In his studies on dropouts in large urban districts, Mr. Balfanz has found that tracking several classroom indicators for individual students and addressing problems in those areas early can prevent later troubles. Attendance rates, behavior, and grades, he concludes, are far more accurate predictors of who will graduate or drop out than test scores, race, or socioeconomic status.

About 40 percent of eventual dropouts could be identified in the 6th grade, he estimates. "The only way to intervene is if we know who the kids are," he said, and are familiar with their records in school.

Mr. Balfanz and his colleagues, like several researchers before them, contend that many students begin to go astray well before they reach high school. Middle schools, he believes, should be the first line of defense in tracking those warning signs and intervening.

"Some kids do OK in middle school, and it's the transition to high school that will get them in trouble," he said. Programs designed to support 9th graders with the transition, however, may not address the difficulties of those students who Mr. Balfanz says are already on their way to becoming dropout statistics.

"Now we can show that for a significant segment of kids, 9th grade doesn't throw them off track," he added, "it finishes them."

By many indications, middle schools are not heeding that message. Researchers and policymakers have pointed to the poor performance of 8th graders on national assessments as evidence that they are not prepared to meet high academic standards. On the 2007 National Assessment of Educational Progress, for example, only about 3 in 10 could demonstrate proficiency in reading and mathematics. Advocates of high school reform often point to the failure of middle schools to prepare students to tackle a challenging secondary-level curriculum.

"Why are schools not systematically monitoring early signs of academic withdrawal?" said Sandra L. Christenson, a professor of educational psychology at the University of Minnesota-Twin Cities in Minneapolis. "If you are systematically monitoring alterable variables, then you can target students for intervention to change their future."

Ms. Christenson helped develop the Check & Connect program more than a decade ago. The intervention program assigns a mentor to students considered at risk academically to check attendance, grades, and other concerns and to work with students and their families to head off school failure. Despite evidence of the success of her program and others like it, Ms. Christenson said, it has not spread to middle schools because of the time and expense. Check & Connect costs about $1,300 per student.

Addressing the Needs of Middle School Students

Although still widely considered the weak link between elementary and secondary education, middle schools have not garnered as much attention as the earlier and later grades, which have begun to benefit from federal initiatives and privately financed school improvement efforts.

Last fall, legislation was introduced in Congress to support a middle-grades clearinghouse, research projects, and grants to districts using instructional models that have been found effective. Those bills were referred to the Senate education committee and a House subcommittee, and could be attached to proposals for reauthorization of the No Child Left Behind Act.

The movement to create schools more responsive to the developmental needs of young adolescents began more than 30 years ago. Then in 1996, American middle and high school students lagged on the Third International Mathematics and Science Study, or TIMSS—results that put a harsh spotlight on the middle grades. The next year, a group of advocates formed the National Forum to Accelerate Middle Grades Reform to help improve curricula, instruction, and research in the field.

Now, the accountability measures required under the federal No Child Left Behind Act, observers say, have been raising the stakes for middle school educators and again putting the focus on academic rigor.

Middle school advocates say that push requires more than an emphasis on test scores.

"While we prepare students for testing, it's also important to prepare them for other aspects of living and knowing," said Drew Sawyer, the principal of Rogers-Herr Middle School.

Here in North Carolina, the 33,000-student Durham school district is working with all its middle schools to do both. Officials here have instituted a number of strategies to ensure consistent monitoring and support of students, particularly those in the middle grades.

As part of its high school completion plan, the district has begun to track students' attendance, discipline records, and academic performance, and it sends that information to schools each month. School counselors and truancy officers have ramped up home visits for students who have missed a significant number of days and haven't responded to phone calls and letters. Local judges volunteer time once a week to hold truancy court for students with patterns of poor attendance, their parents, social workers, and school officials to outline state mandates and the potential consequences of flouting them.

"Truancy is often a symptom of other, underlying family and personal issues, and a lot of times that's brought out in truancy court," said Debra Pitman, the district's assistant superintendent for student-support services. "In truancy court, the problem-solvers are right there in a formal setting, and with a layer of compassion, the message is that this is very serious."

School officials have instituted more effective discipline approaches that have reduced suspension rates, and built formal partnerships with other agencies in Durham to help families get the health, legal, and financial services they need. They have also retrained school counselors to seek out students who need help, rather than waiting for them to knock on their doors. The counselors give extra attention to students who have a history of academic difficulties or attendance problems.

Each middle school offers after-school academic and recreation programs, as well as daily classes to help students catch up in their schoolwork or move ahead with a more challenging curriculum.

The district's dropout rate for seniors has fallen over the past several years—to 4.9 percent for the 2006–07 school year—and is now below the state average.

A School to Watch

With its diverse enrollment—69 percent black, 16 percent white, 10 percent Hispanic, and nearly 40 percent low-income—Rogers-

Herr Middle School has seen results from the district's efforts. Its attendance rate hovers above 96 percent, and it received a "high growth" designation from the state last year for its improved test scores. Last year, it also was recognized as one of North Carolina's "schools to watch" by the National Forum to Accelerate Middle Grades Reform in Champaign, Ill. The designation goes to schools that infuse academic excellence, developmental appropriateness, and democratic education principles.

Each day, students here are welcomed with hugs and handshakes from teachers and administrators—as well as reminders on the dress code and expectations for conduct. First period is "core plus," designed for catching up on classwork or doing extra-credit assignments.

One recent morning, Karine Thate, a 7th grade science teacher, checks a grade book that lists incomplete assignments, projects, and homework for each student. Ms. Thate moves from student to student, reviewing their homework binders, helping them organize their work, and clarifying instructions.

What Makes Middle Schools Work

Higher-performing middle schools share many of the same practices and attributes, concludes a study of 15 New York state middle schools that serve larger-than-average percentages of poor students.

Researchers compared practices at 10 successful middle schools and those at 5 average-performing middle schools with similar demographic profiles and funding levels. They found that the better-performing schools stressed teamwork, collaboration, and common educational goals. Educators at those schools also worked to give students a sense of social and emotional well-being and routinely gathered and analyzed data to help them make decisions about programs and instructional practices.

The study was conducted by Just for the Kids-New York, which is the state affiliate of Just for the Kids, a national nonprofit organization based at the University of Texas at Austin.

By Debra Viadero   February 6, 2008

"Aren't you supposed to show your work?" she asks one boy as she checks his math homework. "This is your chance to change some of your zero grades by giving me a completed assignment," she tells her students just as the chatter grows louder. "You have 15 more minutes," she reminds them. "Use it well."

Several students are doing just that, as they prepare a multimedia presentation for an honors English/language arts class.

Later, during her science class, the teacher helps students produce video presentations that illustrate what they have been learning about the genetic characteristics of fruit flies. The stars of those movies—hundreds of red- and brown-eyed flies—flutter in the glass vials that line the windowsill of the science lab. Illustrations of the flies' life cycle, and the Punnett squares that show the probabilities of the genetic characteristics of their offspring, line the room.

"Raising the fruit flies and making the movie have really helped to bring [the lesson] to life," says Adam Brown, who sits in a computer lab with classmate Lionel Nelson, recording the narration for their movie.

"I've learned a lot about how traits are passed down from generation to generation," Lionel says.

Even this kind of interactive, multimedia project doesn't hold the attention of all students. Several pairs get distracted by the novel features of the software, while others sit idle, seemingly at a loss for what to record after having failed to prepare their scripts. Ms. Thate offers students a chance to catch up after school, but just a handful indicate they will use the extra lab time.

In other classes, similar signs of student indifference are on display. One boy spends much of the school day disrupting classes or distracting others. He loudly sharpens his pencil while the teacher lays out the day's lesson. He tugs at a girl's long hair, and shouts out inappropriate answers. One diligent student in the class complains that the teacher has to spend much of her time attending to the "troublemakers," making the class tedious or boring at times.

The boy's behavior and teachers' concerns about other students are raised later in a daily meeting Ms. Thate has with Ms. Cline and other members of their grade-level team.

"We have some kids who are working real hard to fail," Ms. Cline says. "We just keep trying to find what they're good at and use that to get them more involved. We tell them all the time that we care about them."

That philosophy carries throughout the 6th, 7th, and 8th grade corridors and other corners of the building, too, as is evident in the ease with which students and adults here interact.

Outside the lunchroom, for example, a group of 6th graders chats with Vince Bynum, a police officer assigned to the school, about their classes. Later, the officer shares a laugh with two students who volunteered to pick up trash in front of the school.

The principal's office is a stop-off for students throughout the day, but not because they're in trouble. Several sit at the table in Mr. Sawyer's office to discuss a conflict they have with their classmates. A student who has missed several weeks of school for medical reasons asks the principal to review his new class schedule. Another boy explains an argument he's had with a teacher, trying to convince Mr. Sawyer that there was no good reason for her to reject one of the boy's assignments.

"Now I know you didn't speak to [the teacher] in the same tone you're using now," the principal says, reminding the student to be respectful. He sends him off with some tips for continuing the discussion with the teacher.

Despite the progress, Mr. Sawyer still sees his share of discipline and academic problems.

But he and his colleagues are working at devising the strategies and building the relationships that can help head off those problems for most students.

"We are every other middle school, with the same challenges and celebrations," Mr. Sawyer said. "Our problems are just not as visible because we try to get out ahead of them."

•   •   •

STUDENTS PLAY LEAD ROLE IN DROPOUT PROJECT

BY CATHERINE GEWERTZ
November 19, 2008

A GROUP OF STUDENT LEADERS in Chicago has persuaded the city school system to launch a pilot program designed to reduce the dropout rate by making high school more relevant and responsive to teenagers' needs.

Students from 12 high schools and 7 community groups banded together to form Voices of Youth in Chicago Education, or VOYCE, and conducted a yearlong research project to find out why so many young people leave school and don't attend college.

One of their findings was that students blame themselves, rather than their schools, for the high dropout problem. They also discovered that students disengage from school because they see no connection between their studies and their own lives and futures.

Based on those and other findings, the 409,000-student Chicago school district announced last week that it has agreed to start the first phase of a pilot project in 12 high schools. In 8 of those schools, freshmen will develop personalized graduation plans, and those who are having difficulty will have a chance to participate in "guidance retreats" to get them back on track. The district will also set up a process to allow students to have a say in curriculum reform and teacher training.

At some of the schools, VOYCE leaders will help build student-led leadership teams with teachers and administrators and start a leadership academy to train other students how to bring about positive change in their schools. They will also have "community orientations" for teachers to better acquaint them with the neighborhoods they teach in.

Hennessy Williams, 18, who took part in the research enterprise, said the project sends a message to teenagers everywhere.

"They can change things if they want to," said Mr. Williams, a junior at Kenwood Academy. "But who you talk to about it, and how you do it, matters. You could start a group. You don't just try to change things, but you do the research first. That can make a big difference."

Chicago schools chief executive officer Arne Duncan said in a statement that the district "recognizes that students have an important role to play in their education" and that the pilot represents "the first step in a potential series" of programs to better engage high school students.

. . .

INSTRUCTIONAL MODEL MAY YIELD GAINS FOR ENGLISH-LEARNERS

BY MARY ANN ZEHR
December 5, 2007

NEW YORK. Educators at a small public school for immigrant students at the foot of the Manhattan Bridge here believe its unusual instructional approach—which includes mixing students at various levels of English proficiency—is a key reason why Brooklyn International High School has a graduation rate that outpaces that of many other public schools in New York City.

That model, being used by eight other small high schools for immigrants in this city and one in Oakland, Calif., is supported by a New York City-based nonprofit organization, Internationals Network for Public Schools, which has plans to transplant it to other cities.

The nonprofit was started in 2004 with a grant from the Bill & Melinda Gates Foundation to build on the success of four international high schools that already had been started in the city by helping to expand the number of such schools. Brooklyn International opened its doors in 1994.

The New York educators' enthusiasm is understandable, if the completion rate at Brooklyn International is any measure: eighty percent of its students graduate after four years, while, on average, 60 percent of New York City's students do the same.

Particularly impressive is the school's success with English-language learners. The four-year high school graduation rate in 2007 for students who were still ELLs at graduation was 65 percent; in 2006, the most recent year for which data are available, the city's average four-year graduation rate for ELLs was 26 percent.

While some may question whether English-learners could be shortchanged by attending a school with only other immigrants, Pamela Taranto, the principal of the 392-student school, said that anyone with that view can "look at our results."

Note of Caution

Experts on ELLs sound a note of caution, however. They say that teaching ELLs in groups with mixed levels of English fluency can be effective, but that schools must have a strong professional-development program to prepare teachers to deliver differentiated instruction.

"It's extremely difficult to pull off," said Claude Goldenberg, an education professor at Stanford University who is conducting a study for the U.S. Department of Education's Institute of Education Sciences on differentiated instruction for ELLs.

For example, he said, teachers would have to learn how to give different assignments to different students, vary what questions they ask different students, put students in flexible groups that change throughout the day and school year, and adopt other strategies to teach students of different English-proficiency levels effectively in the same classrooms.

"It's difficult to sustain that," said Mr. Goldenberg.

On the other hand, he said, when ELLs are grouped with students who have similar English skills, the students at the beginning and intermediate levels can get a watered-down curriculum. "Teachers tend to oversimplify because they don't want to frustrate them," he said.

Professional-development is a key part of Brooklyn International's model, according to Ms. Taranto, who said it takes teachers in her school about three years to become adept at carrying out the school's instructional model.

Teachers are assigned in teams of five to work with the same cohort of students, and they often coordinate with one another to facilitate interdisciplinary learning projects. Ninth and tenth graders take all classes together, and for those grades the same teachers stick with the same group of students and team of teachers for two years.

Not 'Scared' to Speak

Students at Brooklyn International highlight a different aspect of the school that they say helps them to acquire English fluency and academic content: the fact that it admits only immigrants. Everyone is an English-learner at the time of enrollment.

Dropout Prevention: Heeding the Early Warning Signs

Students who are at risk for dropping out of high school can be identified as early as 6th grade by key warning signs such as low attendance, little classroom participation, and poor grades in core subjects, according to a study by the National High School Center, a division of the Washington-based American Institutes for Research, a nonprofit organization that conducts research on social and behavioral sciences.

The study also found that 8th graders who fail English or mathematics have a 75 percent chance of dropping out of high school, and it recommends that schools adopt electronic data systems to track students over time.

The data for this report was gathered from studies from multiple nonprofit, academic, and governmental agencies.

By Mary C. Breaden   November 14, 2007

"I don't feel scared to speak English here," said Richard Abreu, a 16-year-old 10th grader from the Dominican Republic, who said he had felt ignored by many other students at the two other New York City schools he attended. "People thought, 'I can't talk to him. He doesn't speak English,'" he recalled.

Stephany Li, a senior, said that when she arrived from China more than five years ago, she was placed in a bilingual program with other Chinese students and didn't mix with other students. "I didn't speak any English at all when I was in junior high," said Ms. Li, who now speaks English with ease.

Brooklyn International students also say they get practice speaking with native speakers of English during required internships in the community during junior year.

With students from 44 countries, the school isn't lacking racial and ethnic diversity, Ms. Taranto noted. "For a lot of our students, they are coming from countries where everyone is like them," she said. "They are very interested in the diversity here."

Classroom Interaction

On a recent fall day, the school's focus on interactive lessons and differentiated instruction was evident in three different classes on core subjects visited by a reporter: a science class for 9th and 10th graders and a social studies class and an English class for seniors.

Dina Begum, a 10th grader from Bangladesh, was a natural leader in her group of four students who were conducting a science experiment comparing the surface tension of tap water and soapy tap water.

"We need a beaker, right?" she said to start the group out.

"What's the title, baby?" she asked when they started making a graph of their data. "Now, let's get to work," she said, when they'd finished the graph and were supposed to write an analysis.

As the only 10th grader in the group and the student with the highest proficiency in English, she was assigned to write two paragraphs analyzing the experiment while the student with the lowest English proficiency was assigned to write two sentences.

In the English class with seniors, students in a group with Koey Chen, a 16-year-old from China, urged her to participate, even though she was reluctant to speak.

The students retold a short story they had read for homework by taking turns saying a couple of sentences about it in a circle—called a "round robin" exercise. Ms. Chen was silent when it was her turn to talk—and a boy started to jump in for her.

"Don't say it for her—ask her a question," said Marco Ma, another student from China, whom the teacher had selected to lead the group.

"I only read up to here," admitted Ms. Chen, pointing to a copy of the short story.

But rather than let her off the hook, Nathaly Cabral, 17, a student from the Dominican Republic, tried to draw her out. "Where did you read up to? What happened there? What was [the character's] reaction to that?" Ms. Cabral asked.

The students relented only when Ms. Chen said the words her teacher had told her permit her to skip her turn: "I pass."

Coverage of new schooling arrangements and classroom improvement efforts is supported by a grant from the Annenberg Foundation.

.   .   .

★ RAISING GRADUATION RATES
IN AN ERA OF HIGH STANDARDS ★

COMMENTARY BY CHERYL ALMEIDA
AND ADRIA STEINBERG
July 30, 2008

IN THE WANING MONTHS of the Bush administration, both public officials and private-sector leaders are demonstrating great interest in addressing the shockingly high dropout rate in many American high schools. In April, U.S. Secretary of Education

Margaret Spellings announced that the U.S. Department of Education will begin requiring all states to calculate graduation rates the same way by the 2012–13 school year.

She made the announcement at the same time that former U.S. Secretary of State Colin Powell was helping launch the America's Promise Alliance's nationwide campaign to combat the problem, an initiative that will convene dropout-prevention summits in 50 states and 50 cities by the end of 2010.

This is all good news. It is time that the simmering concern about the fate of those who never complete high school comes to a boil. It is also time that policies to prevent students from leaving school and to reduce dropout rates be made as high a priority as policies designed to raise overall academic performance to a college-ready standard.

The National Governors Association accelerated this effort three years ago when it pushed states to voluntarily agree to use common measures of dropping out. For years, states had routinely reported graduation rates of 90 percent or higher. We know that the real average for most states is closer to 70 percent. And as Secretary Spellings' announcement indicates, still more progress needs to be made. In the next few years, it will be critical for states to move beyond the important task of implementing new standards for calculating cohort graduation rates, to create a range of incentives, supports, and sanctions that can help more high schools graduate many more students ready for college and careers.

Next-generation accountability systems should redress the single-minded emphasis in current systems on meeting high standards by giving weight to graduation as an equally critical goal.

A blueprint for this policy agenda is taking shape. States are beginning to implement legislation and policies that make graduation rates as important an accountability measure as high academic performance. A growing number of state-level efforts seek to identify and support struggling students early, quickly address poorly performing high schools, and support the creation of new schools and programs that work for struggling and out-of-school youths.

These efforts are as much a part of the college-ready agenda as set-ting and raising academic-performance levels for those who make it through high school.

A number of states are taking the lead. Some, like Georgia and Indiana, have passed new dropout-prevention legislation. Others, including Michigan and Kentucky, have set numeric goals for post-secondary completion. Still others, such as Massachusetts, are building P-16 longitudinal-data systems and beginning to study inefficiencies and leaks in the pipeline that links education to eco-nomic growth, so that graduation rates can be increased and suc-cessful transitions to college maximized.

These first steps are tentative, though. State policymakers worry that the goal of keeping more students in school until they gradu-ate, while also raising expectations for them, may constitute an-other "mission impossible." But new research and lessons from the field and from the states have helped outline a coherent set of policy strategies addressing this problem systematically. It is now up to all states to incorporate this framework into their own poli-cies and practices.

During the past several years, our nonprofit organization, Jobs for the Future, has partnered with Achieve Inc. in an initiative funded by the Carnegie Corporation of New York to study how states might best support such efforts to raise standards and graduation rates. In "Raising Graduation Rates in an Era of High Standards," a report that builds on this work, we call on state policymakers to follow the lead of their most innovative peers and commit to five critical outcomes for their districts, schools, and students. Our work suggests specific steps states can take to focus high school reform efforts on securing the following five outcomes:

• **A high school diploma that signifies college—and work—readiness.** States must ensure equal access for all young people to academically challenging, high-quality high school programs of study—and do that without stifling local and school-based innova-tion and flexibility in curriculum design. To have quality, equity, and consistency in the delivery of a college-prep course of study, states will need to monitor coursetaking patterns, disaggregate data for race and income, include student-transcript data in state data systems, and connect K–12 and postsecondary data systems, so that student progress to and through college can be tracked. Making sure that curricular innovation is not stifled in the quest for consistency will require that states give districts flexibility, holding schools responsible for outcomes while supporting and aiding the innovators who want to create evidence-based instructional programs that will engage particular groups of struggling students and help them succeed.

• **Pathways to graduation and college success for struggling and out-of-school students.** Effective high schools—particularly those for low-income, African-American, and Hispanic youths—tend to be small and to emphasize relationships, relevance, and academic rigor. There are far too few of these, and few vehicles for their development and support. States need to establish these vehicles, as well as the conditions and funding to ensure that such schools are developed or replicated in communities with concentrations of struggling students and dropouts.

North Carolina stands out in this regard for its effort to support partnerships and other means for spurring new school development. The state's New Schools Project is the school-development entity for Gov. Michael F. Easley's ambitious Learn and Earn high schools. It has already created more than 40 new schools whose students can earn both a high school diploma and up to two years of college credit or an associate degree, tuition-free.

• **Turnaround of low-performing high schools.** States need to identify low-performing "dropout factory" high schools, and work with districts to create the conditions and capacities either to turn these schools around or replace them with more-effective options. A few states, such as Florida and Arizona, now provide supports for their lowest-performing schools. These include technical assistance, capacity-building, and funding. Equally important, both states ensure that a lack of reform progress will result in significant state intervention. In an era of limited resources, one of the most important sources of funding for new, effective schools and programs will have to be the replacement of dropout factories with more evidence-based, high-quality options for those schools' students.

• **Increased emphasis on graduation rates and college-readiness in next-generation accountability.** Additional accountability indicators, recognitions, and incentives—starting with a set of "on-track metrics" predictive of high school graduation, such as promotion from 9th to 10th grade, or completion of core courses—can help states encourage schools and districts to hold on to struggling students, get them back on track to a diploma, and increase their readiness for college and careers.

Louisiana's Graduation Index creates incentives for high schools both to keep students enrolled through graduation and to provide a rigorous curriculum through the senior year. Next-generation accountability systems should redress the single-minded emphasis in current systems on meeting high standards by giving weight to graduation as an equally critical goal.

• **Early and continuous support for struggling students.** Research in Chicago and Philadelphia has identified powerful 6th and 9th grade school-based indicators of the likelihood of dropping out, such as academic performance in core courses, credit accumulation, and attendance. If states strengthened their data systems to include such indicators and also helped school districts develop and use accurate early-warning systems to identify off-track students and target interventions early, far more struggling students would get back on track and succeed in high school and beyond.

The time is right for state action to raise graduation rates at the same time that academic-performance expectations are being raised. The public, increasingly concerned about the country's economic standing, is beginning to demand action. And policymakers see clearly the economic imperative of increasing the number of residents with postsecondary credentials. These five state-policy commitments point the way to turning what may seem unattainable into a must-win "mission possible" of making high standards achievable for all students.

CHAPTER 6

Expand Opportunities to Learn

"A truly historic commitment to education—a real commitment—will require new resources and new reforms."

BARACK OBAMA

Manchester, N.H., November 20, 2007

THE ISSUE

We expect students to learn more today than ever before, and many experts agree that additional learning time, particularly for struggling students, is important to gaining knowledge and skills for the 21st century. The typical school day is a throwback to America's agricultural era and is not on par with that of other developed countries around the world. Longer school days or longer school years can help provide additional learning time for students to close the achievement gap. For working parents who have to juggle childcare and work responsibilities, access to high-quality after-school programs will help their children learn and strengthen a broad range of skills.

THE OBAMA PLAN

The Obama-Biden plan includes proposals to:

- **Expand High-Quality After-School Opportunities:** Double funding for the main federal support for after-school programs—the 21st Century Learning Centers program—to serve one million more children each year.

- **Expand Learning Time:** Create a program for states and districts that want to provide additional learning time for students in need.

PERSPECTIVES

BUILDING CONSENSUS ON LEARNING TIME

EXPANDING LEARNING TIME

HIGH-QUALITY AFTER-SCHOOL PROGRAMS
TIED TO TEST-SCORE GAINS

STUDENT ENGAGEMENT

. . .

BUILDING CONSENSUS ON LEARNING TIME

BY CATHERINE GEWERTZ
September 24, 2008

UNDER ENORMOUS PRESSURE to prepare students for a successful future—and fearful that standard school hours don't offer enough time to do so—educators, policymakers, and community activists are adding more learning time to children's lives.

"This issue is hot right now," said Bela P. Shah, a senior program associate for after-school initiatives at the National League of Cities' Institute for Youth, Education, and Families. "There's a real understanding that we have to do more, and that everyone has to take responsibility for it."

Twenty-five years ago, the still-resonant report *A Nation at Risk* urged schools to add more time—an hour to the usual six-hour day and 20 to 40 days to the typical 180-day year—to ward off a "rising tide of mediocrity" in American education. Today, in city agencies and school district offices, at statehouses and on the national stage, leaders are engaged in a renewed effort to do just that.

"Everywhere I go, people are talking about this now," said An-Me Chung, a program officer for the Charles Stewart Mott Foundation, which has financed school-community partnerships and after-school programs since the 1930s. The Flint, Mich.-based philanthropy has also taken a leading role in convening scholars, practitioners, and policymakers to rethink the role time should play in learning.

"They're stepping back and taking a much more holistic approach than they did even eight years ago," Ms. Chung said of those who have been discussing expanded learning. "They realize we've got to think about time and learning in more than just a piecemeal way."

Hundreds of Initiatives

The idea of finding more time for learning has generated a hotbed of activity nationwide. A July study for the Center for American Progress, a Washington think tank, found that more than 300 initiatives to extend learning time were launched between 1991 and 2007 in high-poverty and high-minority schools in 30 states. A compilation of extended-day activity at the state level by the Denver-based Education Commission of the States found more than 50 efforts since 2000.

Adding learning time takes many forms. It can mean freeing students from the clock by letting them complete assignments on a computer, in their pajamas, at 2 A.M., or letting them take five years to finish high school, as the Boston district allows. It can mean forging better links between children's schools and the many learning experiences in their cities, as Providence, R.I., has done, by building "afterzones" of networked after-school programs for its middle-schoolers, from sports and fashion design to college guidance counseling, and providing the wheels to get them there.

Most often, retooling time means extending the school day or school year to accommodate the burgeoning list of skills and areas of knowledge students need to thrive as adults.

'Only Way to Go'

At Grove Patterson Academy, a regular public K–8 school in Toledo, Ohio, an eight-hour day and a 192-day year afford time for all 400 children to have 90 minutes of daily, uninterrupted reading, to study Spanish or German, to explore music and art, to engage in sports, and to work with mathematics specialists.

The extra time—the equivalent of 49 more days in the year—makes possible an interdisciplinary-learning approach that Principal Gretchen E. Bueter calls invaluable. Children do math problems in German, boost their Spanish and geography skills in social studies class, and learn graphing and numeric value in music. Teachers have daily planning time together to coordinate coursework across the curriculum.

"I feel this is the only way to go," Ms. Bueter said. "This is a better way of preparing children to go out there and be ready for whatever they do."

Among other high-profile efforts to extend learning time:

- New York City and its teachers' union added 37.5 minutes a day to the first four days of the week so teachers can tutor underperforming students in small groups.

- Eight communities are seeking grants from the Mott Foundation to implement a new form of expanded learning that envisions a "seamless learning experience" obtained inside and outside the schoolhouse, and supported by a web of community services.

- In Massachusetts, a widely watched, 3-year-old initiative to expand learning time gives districts about $1,300 per pupil to add 30 percent more time to the school year. Leaders of the program said they are advising at least seven other states interested in doing something similar.

- "People see that we can't consistently achieve our goals inside the usual time frame," said Chris Gabrieli, the co-chairman of the National Center on Time and Learning, which advises the 26 schools implementing the Massachusetts Expanded Learning Time initiative in 2008–09. "We're way short of the mark."

With backing from both national teachers' unions, U.S. Sen. Edward M. Kennedy, D-Mass., introduced legislation last month that would provide federal funding for districts or schools wishing to follow the Massachusetts example. Legislation sponsored last fall by U.S. Rep. Donald Payne, D-N.J., contains similar ideas.

The time issue has even worked its way into the presidential race. The platform of the Democratic nominee, Sen. Barack Obama of Illinois, calls for high-quality summer and after-school programs. Two coalitions that formed to keep education issues visible in the 2008 race list extended learning time among their priorities.

This past summer, the National Center for Summer Learning at Johns Hopkins University in Baltimore launched a $5.2 million public-policy campaign to promote funding for summer programs, especially for children whose families cannot provide the array of educational experiences children of wealthier parents enjoy.

The campaign has been publicizing findings by Johns Hopkins sociologist Karl Alexander, who traces two-thirds of the achievement gap between students of less-advantaged and more-affluent backgrounds to summer learning loss by poorer children. It also cites research that suggests children with few good summer-activity options have more health problems, such as obesity and diabetes.

Ron Fairchild, the executive director of the center, believes that the rush of activity on the local, state, and national levels shows that the importance of out-of-school time to children's learning is finally getting the recognition it deserves.

"We're starting to see a real tipping point on this issue," he told a group of advocates who gathered in Washington on July 10 to lobby Congress for funding.

On-and-Off Debate

Numbers have no doubt helped tip the debate. The Washington-based Council of Chief State School Officers found that in 2006, 21 states required a school day of less than five hours or had no requirement. Only three states mandated school years longer than 180 days.

Education Resource Strategies, a Watertown, Mass.-based nonprofit consulting firm, studied in 2006 how many hours per year students spent in school in 10 urban districts. The results varied from

914 in Chicago to 1,274 in Houston. And that's what researchers call "allocated school time," which includes lunch, passing periods between classes, and the like. Not all allocated school time is class time, and even less is high-quality instructional time, experts say.

Urban schoolchildren didn't always spend so little time in class. Studies show that in the mid-1800s, some big cities kept schools open more than 250 days a year. New York City's schools were open year-round, with only a three-week break in August. But by the turn of the 20th century, the urban school year grew shorter as middle-class parents began to insist on vacation time, while rural school calendars, often interrupted by farming demands and shortened by lack of funding, grew longer. By the middle of the 20th century, most U.S. schools had settled into the late-summer-to-late-spring standard, with a solid block of summer vacation.

In *A Nation at Risk*, the National Commission on Excellence in Education, formed by then-U.S. Secretary of Education Terrel H. Bell, said improving American education would require higher expectations, better teaching, and better curricula. But it would also take "significantly more time," the commission said, used more effectively.

Adding more school time has been discussed and tried intermittently since the report's release in 1983. "Prisoners of Time," a 1994 report by another federal panel, reiterated calls for a longer school day and year, saying time is the "unacknowledged design flaw" in American education, and must support learning, not limit it.

But the idea has taken hold with particular fervor in the past decade, driven in large part by the academic-standards movement, which has sought to define what students should know, and heightened attention to achievement gaps between students of different races, ethnicities, and socioeconomic backgrounds, which showed how far many children still had to go.

The federal No Child Left Behind Act, signed into law in January 2002, added urgency to the rethinking of time, observers say, by dangling consequences over schools that don't progress briskly enough. The globalizing economy, meanwhile, popularized the idea that to thrive, young people must master not only core academics, but also a set of "21st-century skills" such as critical thinking and teamwork.

Also fueling the rethinking of time was the expansion of federally funded 21st Century Community Learning Centers, which seek to use after-school time for a blend of academics and enrichment. The program grew from $40 million annually in 1998 to $1 billion a year by 2002, and has retained support near that level ever since, despite attempts by President Bush to cut it.

Time in Charter Schools

The rise of charter schools also has given educators something to think about. Two-thirds of those public schools use their freedom from most regulations to adopt longer days or longer years, according to the Center for Education Reform, a Washington group that supports and tracks charters and other forms of school choice.

Experts often point to schools run by the Knowledge Is Power Program, or KIPP, as an example of what more time can do. KIPP's overwhelmingly low-income students have made strong gains in a rigorous, college-preparatory program that spans 8½ hours a day, every other Saturday, and three weeks of the summer.

The push to add more time to learning also has accelerated a cross-fertilization of the education, youth-development, and after-school worlds. Recreation and job-training programs often add

---

Accumulated Effects of Summer Learning Loss

Researcher Karl Alexander and his colleagues at Johns Hopkins University have tracked the achievement trajectories of more than 700 Baltimore schoolchildren who started 1st grade in 1982. They found that learning gaps between low-income children and their middle-income peers widened during the summer months because of differences in learning opportunities.

academic help, for instance. More schools are seeking to replicate for children of low-income families the rich array of learning experiences—from art class to internships—that better-off children receive outside the school walls.

"Why should we think about the learning day as ending at the school door?" said Milton Goldberg, who was the executive director of the National Commission on Excellence in Education, directed the panel that produced the "Prisoners of Time" report, and remains a leader in the movement to rethink learning time.

"People aren't just talking about having more learning time," he said. "They're talking about a fundamentally different conception of when and where kids learn."

The C.S. Mott Foundation convened leaders of the education and after-school worlds in 2005 to help define that new conception of learning.

In a 2007 report, "A New Day for Learning," the Mott panel urged erasing the distinction between school and after-school, and creating a "seamless" experience that would impart academic, cultural, and civic learning, along with such skills as critical thinking and teamwork. It would extend beyond the schoolhouse, with "no final bell." That approach requires intense, communitywide collaboration, the report said, and "a total rethinking of purposes, practices, and personnel."

The foundation has invited eight school district–community partnerships to apply for grants to build learning systems that embody those principles. Winners are expected to be announced this fall.

Most of the recent expanded-time efforts share some core beliefs. One is that children need more time and opportunity to learn what they need to know. Another is that more time must mean new modes of learning—not just longer vocabulary lists. The initiatives also seem to acknowledge that schools can't do it alone. Educators have long linked up with community groups to extend and enrich students' learning, as evidenced by the century-old Community Schools movement. But those connections are cropping up far more often in schools not formally a part of that coalition.

Even with those tenets in common, though, the initiatives vary in philosophy and approach.

One type operates as an academic intervention for the lowest-performing students. In the Miami-Dade County, Fla., district's former School Improvement Zone, for instance, struggling schools operated on a longer day and year, and the extra time was dedicated exclusively to core academic subjects.

Another type operates as a blend of academics and enrichment, with the primary vision of building well-rounded adults by offering arts, sports, cultural and relational experiences, vocational training, and academic help. Such programs are commonly offered by community groups, alone or in partnership with schools, and may occur during or after the typical school day.

Other extended-time efforts, such as the Massachusetts initiative, are fundamental school redesigns that put the school district squarely in charge of improving performance by aligning the enrichment and academic components. Unlike in some programs, all children in the school must participate.

Randi Weingarten, the president of the American Federation of Teachers, said that if teachers have an integral role in shaping the additional learning time, both students and teachers can be richly rewarded. Students would have time to approach learning differently—in small groups, for instance, or in a more hands-on way—and teachers would build stronger skills and experience more job satisfaction.

"It's not just someone saying, 'We're going to add time to the day, and you're going to have to work it,'" Ms. Weingarten said. "It can be a hugely professional and collegial practice that builds their capacity and is a big morale booster."

Staggering Schedules

Extending time doesn't necessarily mean all teachers would work longer hours, she added. At a New York charter middle school run jointly by the city and the United Federation of Teachers, the local AFT affiliate, the additional hours are covered on a staggered schedule, she said.

Adding time can be expensive and politically tricky, said Elena Silva, a senior policy analyst for the Washington-based think tank Education Sector. She examined the additional-time issue in a 2007 paper, "On the Clock."

A longer school year can run into resistance from certain business interests, such as the amusement-park industry, that employ many teenagers and depend on tourism for revenue, Ms. Silva said, and from middle-class parents who seek more time with their children and resent the disruption to vacations.

A longer day tends to draw less opposition, she said, although high school athletics departments often consider it a problem because it cuts into traditional practice times.

Mr. Gabrieli of the National Center on Time and Learning said schools in the Massachusetts initiative have found a longer day to be more cost-efficient than a longer year.

Expanding Learning Time

"Expanding Learning Time in Action: Initiatives in High-Poverty and High-Minority Schools and Districts"

A report released July 21 profiles more than 300 initiatives across the country that are all aimed at expanding learning time in schools with large concentrations of disadvantaged students.

Researchers at the Center for American Progress, a Washington-based think tank, spent more than two years ferreting out school-, district-, and state-level efforts to lengthen the school day, week, or year by at least 30 percent. The 300 initiatives they identified, which are spread across 30 states, all began between 1991 and 2007.

The study found that the schools, many of which are charter schools, use the extra time in a variety of ways, including mentoring, study of core academic subjects, enrichment, and workforce training.

By Debra Viadero   July 30, 2008

Cost is "absolutely the first thing that comes up" when policy-makers consider adding time, Ms. Silva said.

Another 2008 study for the Center for American Progress, also financed by the Broad Foundation, found that the annual cost of adding 30 percent more time to a school schedule ranged from $287 to $720 per pupil, depending on whether the extra time was staffed with paraprofessionals or with certified employees on a salaried basis. It could be lower if current staffing is reallocated or a stipend system is used, the study says, and higher if newly hired certified staff members are used.

Karen Hawley Miles, the paper's co-author and the executive director of Education Resource Strategies, said schools typically find that they have to spend about 16 percent more to boost time by 30 percent.

One of the concerns sparked by the movement to add time is that it risks simply being an extension of ineffective instruction.

"There are some principals and superintendents who think that more time on task means more of what is already happening," said Lucy N. Friedman, the president of The After-School Corp., or TASC, a nonprofit group in New York City that is managing a new initiative this year to expand time by 30 percent in 11 schools there. "We think kids need a much broader approach to learning."

Youth Workers' Role

Some leaders in the after-school sector worry that their deep expertise in youth development will be left behind in the accelerating dialogue about extended time, at a great cost to children.

"Youth workers have a lot to offer in this current debate. But we'd better hurry—I see a fast-moving train here, and time may be running out," Jane Quinn wrote in a column last year for the publication *Youth Today*. Ms. Quinn is the assistant executive director for community schools at the New York City-based Children's Aid Society, which provides a wide range of services to children and families, on and off school sites. It operates 22 Community Schools jointly with the city's department of education.

Ellen S. Gannett, the director of Wellesley College's National Institute on Out-of-School Time, recalled getting a sinking feeling when she visited an extended-day program in Florida and saw middle schoolers being lectured by a teacher at 4:30 P.M. When she asked a staff member when the students might be able to interact, or learn in more animated ways, she was told that those things could happen when they left the building at 5:30.

"Using time without a sense of personal, relational connection is a big red flag for me," Ms. Gannett said. "Spending afternoons alone at computers without connecting with friends or a caring adult. This is when I get nervous."

Those involved in expanded learning efforts are well aware that such programs are a work in progress. But the movement's promise is starting to bring together people from fields that devote themselves to children, but haven't always worked closely together.

"We have realized that if we are going to make a differences in the lives of kids, we have to help them succeed in school," said Ms. Chung of the Mott Foundation. "School, after-school, and youth development can't do it alone, nor should they have to. We are all educators. We need to get out of those silos. And there is a real effort to do that."

. . .

HIGH-QUALITY AFTER-SCHOOL PROGRAMS TIED TO TEST-SCORE GAINS

BY DEBRA VIADERO
November 28, 2007

DISADVANTAGED STUDENTS who regularly attend top-notch after-school programs end up, after two years, academically far ahead of peers who spend more out-of-school time in unsupervised activities, according to findings from an eight-state study of those programs.

Known as the Promising Afterschool Programs study, the new research examined 35 programs serving 2,914 students in 14 communities stretching from Bridgeport, Conn., to Seaside, Calif. The programs, all of which had been operating at least three years when the study began, were selected because of a record of success.

For advocates of after-school programs, the results offer a counterpoint to a controversial 2005 evaluation of the 21st Century Community Learning Centers program, a federal initiative that finances after-school enrichment programs for 1.3 million elementary and middle school students nationwide.

Conducted by the Princeton, N.J.-based Mathematica Policy Research Inc., the earlier study found that the federally funded programs provided no special learning boost and may even have led to a slight statistical increase in some negative behaviors.

"My hope is that this research can really put to rest the research by Mathematica and really show that after-school programs are making a difference for the children that are participating," said Jennifer Rinehart, the vice president for policy and research for the Washington-based Afterschool Alliance, which is working to circulate the new results.

But some scholars caution that the latest study, which was underwritten by the Charles Stewart Mott Foundation of Flint, Mich., could run up against criticism, too, in ongoing debates over federal spending on after-school programs. One problem cited was that researchers used as a comparison group students who attend after-school programs sporadically, suggesting that those students might have been less motivated at the outset than students who regularly attend such programs.

"What it told me is that kids who are different at baseline are even more different two years later," said Mark Dynarski, who led the Mathematica evaluation. "That's not evidence of effectiveness."

Focus on Quality

In the new study, researchers divided students into three groups: a "program only" group of students who attended their after-school program two to three days a week and did nothing else outside of school; a "program plus" group who visited the after-school programs two to three days a week and also took part in sports, church programs, music lessons, or other extracurricular activities; and a "low supervision" group who dropped in on a mix of after-school activities from one to three days a week.

The researchers found, over the course of the three-year project, that the more engaged students were in supervised after-school activities, the better they did on a range of academic, social, and behavioral outcomes.

For instance, 3rd and 4th graders in the "program plus" group tallied gains on standardized mathematics tests that were 20 percentile points higher than those of the children who rarely went. The frequent attenders also made more progress in developing sound work habits, task persistence, and better social skills, and in reducing negative behaviors, such as skipping school or fighting.

The 6th and 7th grade pupils who regularly attended after-school programs outpaced the math learning gains their "low supervision" counterparts made by 12 percentile points by the end of the study period. The "program" and "program plus" groups also reported reduced rates of drug and alcohol use, compared with students with spottier attendance.

"What makes these findings interesting, and maybe surprising to some people, is that the math gains are occurring in programs that are not specifically targeted to academic skills," said lead author Deborah Lowe Vandell, the chairwoman of the education department at the University of California, Irvine. "Children were developing persistence, focus, and engagement, and we believe those are the kinds of skills that maybe children take to school with them and that may contribute to their math gains."

In designing the Promising Programs study, Ms. Vandell said, she set out to address some of what critics saw as shortcomings in the Mathematica report. Critics and advocates complained, for example, that the earlier study fell short because it involved programs that were young or varied in quality.

So Ms. Vandell and her research partners—Elizabeth R. Reisner of Policy Studies Associates Inc. of Washington and Kim M. Pierce of UC Irvine—zeroed in on the best programs. Not all the programs were funded under 21st Century Schools or based in schools.

The research team selected 35 programs serving low-income elementary and middle-school students from among 200 that were nominated for their successful track records.

"Other work that I have done looking at the association between varying quality programs and child development was suggesting that higher-quality programs were where you expected better outcomes," said Ms. Vandell. "We do see gains there that we don't see otherwise."

Ms. Vandell acknowledged that the comparison-group issue that Mr. Dynarski raised posed a "limitation" for her study, but

---

Student Engagement

"Assessing School Engagement: A Guide for Out-of-School Time Program Practitioners"

Students who are not engaged in school are at a higher risk of poor academic achievement, but leaders of after-school programs may not have a good understanding of how to captivate those they serve.

The three types of engagement are behavioral, emotional, and cognitive, according to a new guide for assessing student engagement from Child Trends, a Washington-based research organization.

Out-of-schooltime programs have also been found to increase student interest if they offer mentoring, community service, academic tutoring, and "life skills" training.

"In general, students are more likely to be engaged if they have support from adults at their school, challenging and interesting tasks, adequate structure, support for autonomy, opportunities to learn with peers, and opportunities for active learning," the report says.

By Linda Jacobson   November 5, 2008

said her team took steps to minimize potential bias. One way was to compare students' gains with their own previous performance, rather than looking at the overall achievement levels of the various groups.

Funding at Issue

The Mathematica study began in 2000, four years after President Clinton launched the 21st Century Community Learning Centers program and two years after the program was repurposed to provide a more academic focus.

The study became a target of criticism, in part, because President Bush used its early findings to justify his call in 2002 for a 40 percent cut in that program, which at that time was funded at about $1 billion. Congress later agreed to provide $981 million for the program and it has remained at that annual funding level ever since.

The findings from the new study are in keeping with a growing body of research linking after-school programs to gains in social and emotional outcomes for students in organized activities after school.

For instance, a review of 73 studies published this year by the Chicago-based Collaborative for Academic, Social, and Emotional Learning looked specifically at programs aimed at developing youths' personal and social skills and found that such programs could be linked to a wide range of improvement in students.

Compared with their control-group counterparts, that analysis concluded, program participants experienced greater increases in self-esteem and self-confidence, more decreases in problem behaviors, and improved grades and test scores.

But the sizes of the effects in the Promising Practices study are especially dramatic. The 20-percentile-point gain that "program plus" elementary students made, relative to the "low supervision" group, works out to an effect size of .73. That's more than three times the learning boost that educators get by reducing an elementary school class by eight students, according to Ms. Vandell's research. And that, in Mr. Dynarski's view, may be cause for skepticism.

"How do you get dramatic increases in effects from something that's not even school?" he asked. "You're in it a couple of hours a week or a couple of hours a day, but the activities you're experiencing are very fragmented."

Ms. Vandell said those effect sizes look large in part because the gap was widening over time between the program students and the "low supervision" group. "You have to remember, these were students who were either hanging out with friends or home alone with siblings for two to three days a week," she said of the latter group.

Though the final report from the new study has not yet been published in an academic journal, researchers last month visited Capitol Hill to share the data with federal lawmakers.

The spending measure for health and education programs that President Bush vetoed earlier this month included a $100 million increase for after-school programs, the first such proposed increase in years, according to advocates. They credit the results emerging from the new study for helping to turn the tide in funding prospects for the federal program.

CHAPTER 7

Recruit, Prepare, Retain, and Reward America's Teachers

"We know that from the moment our children step into a classroom, the single most important factor in determining their achievement is not the color of their skin or where they come from; it's not who their parents are or how much money they have. It's who their teacher is."

BARACK OBAMA

Manchester, N.H., November 20, 2007

THE ISSUE

Teachers play a central role in student achievement, yet the teaching profession is plagued by a multitude of problems. Uneven standards of preparation, low pay, and difficult working conditions are among the factors contributing to high turnover and shortages in hard-to-staff areas and subjects. With two million teachers entering the workforce in the next decade, it's time to fundamentally transform the way we recruit, prepare, retain, and reward our nation's teachers.

THE OBAMA PLAN

To attract and keep competent, effective teachers, Obama and Biden offer rich opportunities for professional growth and career development.

- **Recruit Teachers:** Create new Teacher Service Scholarships that will cover four years of undergraduate or two years of graduate teacher education, including high-quality alternative programs for mid-career recruits in exchange for teaching for at least four years in a high-need field or location.

- **Prepare Teachers:** Require all schools of education to be accredited. Obama and Biden will also create a voluntary national performance assessment so we can be sure that every new educator is trained and ready to walk into the classroom and start teaching effectively. Obama and Biden will also create Teacher Residency Programs that will supply 30,000 exceptionally well-prepared recruits to high-need schools.

- **Retain Teachers:** Support our teachers by expanding mentoring programs that pair experienced teachers with new recruits. They will also provide incentives to give teachers paid common planning time so they can collaborate to share best practices.

- **Reward Teachers:** Promote new and innovative ways to increase teacher pay that are developed with teachers, not imposed on them. Districts will be able to design programs that reward with a salary increase accomplished educators who serve as mentors to new teachers. Districts can reward teachers who work in underserved places like rural areas and inner cities. And if teachers consistently excel in the classroom, that work can be valued and rewarded as well.

. . .

ASPIRING TEACHERS
TAKE UP RESIDENCE

BY VAISHALI HONAWAR
October 14, 2008

BOSTON. Each of the past five years, a group of new teachers has been entering some of Boston's toughest schools knowing almost exactly what they can expect and what's expected of them.

That's because they've already spent a year in those buildings, observing and teaching classes under the watchful eye of a specially trained master teacher. They have developed a solid understanding of the academic and disciplinary issues they might confront. And if they need guidance, they know mentor teachers are on hand to help.

The teachers are graduates of the Boston Teacher Residency program, a yearlong, selective preparation route that trains aspiring teachers, many of them career-changers, to take on jobs in some of the city's highest-needs schools.

The program, which fits neither of the two most common types of teacher preparation—alternative routes and traditional teacher education programs—is modeled along the lines of a medical residency that pairs classroom training with practical experience.

According to the program's director, Jesse Solomon, himself a former teacher from Boston, the expertise needed to create excellent teachers already exists in the nation's schools. That realization, and the fact that "we do not believe that it is one element that makes for a great teacher, but a combination of elements," have resulted in a program built around some of the very best practices known to teacher education today.

Mr. Solomon ticks off a few: a rigorous, master's-level grounding in teacher coursework, a yearlong clinical practicum designed to bridge theory and practice, mentoring support for first-year teachers, and preparation in self-reflection and collaborative teaching.

In recent months, teacher education experts have turned the spotlight on teacher residencies as one of the most promising routes for preparing effective educators. Besides the Boston initiative, similar programs are now running in Chicago and in two districts outside Denver, Adams 12 Five Star Schools and Mapleton.

Teacher education experts have turned the spotlight on teacher residencies as one of the most promising routes for preparing effective educators.

New programs are expected to begin next June in Chattanooga and Memphis, Tenn.; Denver; New York City; and Philadelphia, said Aneesa Listak, the executive director of the Urban Teacher Residency Institute. Based in Chicago, the institute was established last year and offers training for groups aiming to start such programs.

Ms. Listak said she has been approached by Ohio and Tennessee education officials interested in forming such programs statewide.

New research shows positive effects of the programs. A study released last month by the Aspen Institute, a Washington think tank, found that 90 percent of the Boston graduates were still teaching after three years, and that more than half the recruits were from racial- and ethnic-minority groups. Also last month, the National Council for Accreditation of Teacher Education released a report calling on traditional teacher education programs to embrace residencies.

What has further fueled interest in urban residency programs is a provision in the newly reauthorized federal Higher Education Act calling for $300 million that could potentially be tapped by teacher-preparation programs and school districts to set up such residencies.

The funding, if appropriated, could help remove one of the deterrents to the spread of such programs: high startup costs. Proponents, though, are quick to point out that the costs are neutralized and even transformed into savings for districts in the long run because of the higher teacher-retention rates.

In Boston, said Mr. Solomon, it costs about $3,000 to find and recruit a resident and just under $30,000 to prepare one. That includes a stipend of $11,000 for each resident, health insurance, and tuition. The resident repays a portion of the tuition only if he or she leaves before teaching for three years.

Observers say one factor that has perhaps been crucial to the success of the Boston program is that it operates independently of the school district—something that is true of the residency programs in Chicago and near Denver as well.

"You have to find those third-party groups that are established and work well enough with the district to create [successful programs]," said Tom Carroll, the president of the National Commission on Teaching and America's Future, a Washington-based advocacy group. "If the university tries to do it, it becomes a variation of a program in the university, or if a district does it, it becomes embedded in other district programs."

Most of the upcoming residency programs, Ms. Listak points out, with the exception of Denver's, will be operated by independent groups.

While it remains to be seen if a district-run model will work, the current "one foot in, one foot out" model is useful, she said, because the programs can leverage change even as they work with school districts that tend to move more slowly. Sustainability of programs run by districts can also be threatened by funding problems and changes in leadership, Ms. Listak added.

The program in Boston originated from the public school system and was housed at the Boston Plan for Excellence, a local education foundation that works in close partnership with the 57,000-student district on professional development for teachers and principals. The startup money came from Strategic Grant Partners, a local foundation.

Under an agreement with the Boston Teacher Residency, the district has paid an increasing proportion of the cost each year, culminating with a 60 percent share in the fourth year. This year, it laid out $2 million.

The program, which is run by many former teachers, recruits and trains teacher-residents on its own, but works closely with the district to place them during their practicums and then as teachers in the city's schools.

Carol Johnson, the superintendent of the Boston schools, says she is encouraged by reports that the program is helping create a diverse workforce of committed teachers in some of the schools with the greatest needs.

"The marketplace here is very competitive when it comes to recruiting teachers of color," she said.

But, Ms. Johnson added, she is waiting for results of a study exploring the residency graduates' effect on student achievement, due next year. "The external evaluation will answer the most important question: whether or not student performance is improving," she said.

Meanwhile, though, anecdotal evidence is plentiful that urban-residency teachers do better in their first year than new teachers prepared by other routes.

Principal Deb Socia of Lilla G. Frederick Pilot Middle School says she finds that new residency graduates have skill levels more like those of second-year teachers.

"The [residents'] preparation has been fabulous, and they have great success with stepping into teaching," she said. "You don't even find that with traditional teacher programs, whose graduates don't necessarily feel confident stepping into an environment like ours."

"All our [Boston Teacher Residency] graduates are stepping up to leadership roles in the building," said Principal Margaret Bledsoe of Charlestown High School, which now has six graduates of the program and six residents on campus. "They are all really strong teachers."

"All our [Boston Teacher Residency] graduates are stepping up to leadership roles in the building."

The urban residency is so popular that Boston schools compete to host residents each year. Many graduates find jobs at the schools they train in.

And because there are typically several residents and graduates at almost every participating school, as well as mentor teachers, the program fosters a constant sharing and camaraderie between its alumni and residents. Those characteristics make for a collaborative learning atmosphere.

Amy Piacitelli, a history teacher at Charlestown High School, has been teaching for 14 years. This year, she's mentoring resident Jawuan Meeks. Ms. Piacitelli finds the experience enriching, she said, because "I like working with other people. . . . Having another person to talk to, to brainstorm with, is really great."

"It is all about building relationships," said residency graduate Katie Reinke, who quit a job writing medical manuals and moved across the country from San Diego to join the program.

She graduated in 2006 and now teaches English at Charlestown High, where she is also a mentor teacher to resident Justin Norton. Ms. Reinke did her resident practicum at Charlestown, and the teacher who mentored her during her practicum is in a classroom next door. "I feel like I can go to her for advice anytime," she said.

Each participating school has a site director who coordinates all residents. Two field directors divide their time visiting all 14 host schools in the program this school year, offering guidance and support when needed.

Ms. Socia says that one of the aspects of the program she loves is knowing that a support network of field and site coordinators is around all the time, willing to provide their expertise in solving problems that might arise. Their counsel, she says, extends even to issues like student attendance, which has been a problem at her school.

All first-year teachers in Boston public schools are assigned mentors, but Mr. Solomon says his program offers professional-development courses and additional support to graduates by sending in coaches when needed. For example, if a mentor assigned to a math graduate does not have a matching content-area background, the residency program would send in a math induction coach.

Each Friday morning, 75 residents, who already have their undergraduate degrees, meet for classes at the University of Massachusetts Boston, set on picturesque Boston Harbor. The residents have been attending classes here since July—two months before Boston schools opened.

At a seminar one recent Friday, they discuss their experiences of the week in their precollegiate classrooms before breaking up into more subject- and grade-specific classes, which are taught by expert practitioners, including former and current Boston teachers, and area university professors.

Guided by Hollee Freeman, one of the program's two field managers, the residents first talk in small groups, then as a single class, about what they learned in each of their classrooms and what they might do differently when they teach themselves. They seek the advice of their peers on issues they faced in the classroom.

At her table, Danielle Berger, a resident at McCormick Middle School, says she worries about how to handle discipline issues in her special education class.

"I wonder how much of the [problems] are built into a special education classroom and how much can be changed," she wonders out loud. Other residents at her table offer suggestions and share similar experiences.

Mr. Norton tells the group at his table that his mentor says he needs to pay more attention to how she handles issues in the classroom.

Like most residents here, Mr. Norton, 28, is a career-changer. He worked in the admissions office at Tufts University and wanted to try something more challenging, he says. That's when he started thinking about a career as a teacher.

He came across the Boston Teacher Residency program in a flier and thought it would be a perfect match. "I wanted something that wasn't going to put me into a class right away," he said.

On a typical day, Mr. Norton gets to Charlestown High at 6:30 A.M. He and Ms. Reinke talk about the day ahead. When school starts, he spends three periods in Ms. Reinke's class and one in a special education class.

All residents receive dual certification in special education because, Mr. Solomon says, one in five of the district's students is classified as having disabilities.

For now, Mr. Norton spends a good part of his time observing Ms. Reinke teach. It is still early in the year, but as the months go by, he will take on more jobs in the classroom, and by spring, he will have assumed half the teaching workload.

At the end of each day, Mr. Norton and Ms. Reinke get back together to review and assess his progress. This is the time when he can question her about why she may have handled certain situations the way she did, and when she can offer him feedback on areas he needs to work on.

Ms. Reinke says she believes candidates who opt to go through the program plan to stay in the profession.

"It is very clear, even when you read the literature from [the program], that there's an urgency there to keep teachers in the building," which, she said, ends up attracting only those who are seriously committed to the job.

As for herself, Ms. Reinke definitely does not miss writing those medical manuals. In her third year of teaching now, she cannot imagine doing any other job.

"I get up at 5:30 each morning," she said, "but there is not a single day that I feel like I don't want to go to work."

. . .

TIERED LICENSING SYSTEMS
USED TO HELP TEACHER QUALITY

BY BESS KELLER
December 19, 2007

MICHIGAN SCHOOL LEADERS announced this fall that they were aiming for a wholesale redesign of a system that mostly gets minor adjustments from states: teacher licensing.

Schools chief Michael P. Flanagan has proposed going to a system with three, rather than the current two, tiers of licensing. Moreover, teachers would progress from level to level only by a performance assessment, not the more standard additional courses and workshops. The proposal is part of a sweeping attempt to jack up teacher quality in the Great Lakes State.

"We think we have to raise the bar on what teachers are expected to do and turn teaching into the profession it is," said Sally Vaughn, the Michigan education department's chief academic officer.

Michigan is not alone in its interest in three-level licensure. In the past few years, Delaware, New Mexico, and Wisconsin have made such a switch, though each with somewhat different aims.

As states explore how to get, keep, and improve the practice of teachers, one popular change has been to do away with lifetime licenses so that state officials can enforce requirements for professional development. A few states, though, are looking to foster bigger improvements through licensing.

New Mexico is a prominent example. In 2003, the legislature enacted changes that included tying minimum salary levels to three teacher classifications. A "provisional" teacher can advance to level 2 only after taking part in a mentoring program for beginners and putting in three to five years of successful classroom experience.

Stricter Requirements

Like New Mexico, many states have added mentoring requisites to their licensing systems as a way of ensuring that districts give new teachers help. A smaller number, following the lead of pioneering Connecticut, have set up ways beyond the standard classroom observations to gauge whether a teacher is ready to take on the responsibilities of a classroom.

In New Mexico, for example, in those first five years of teaching, teachers must each submit a "professional-development dossier" that demonstrates to their principals, mentoring teachers, and two independent reviewers that they have the teaching skills identified by the state. Contents may include lesson plans, reflections on teaching, and assessments showing student-learning gains. If a teacher cannot satisfy those requirements, he or she cannot remain.

To go from level 2 to 3 under New Mexico's system, teachers must have another three years in the classroom and go through a similar portfolio process, though greater skill is expected. They

---

States With Three-Tier Licensing

- Delaware
- Iowa
- Nebraska
- Illinois
- Kansas
- New Mexico
- Indiana
- Maine
- Wisconsin

Source: Education Week 2007

must also have earned a master's degree or advanced certification from the National Board for Professional Teaching Standards.

Level 3 teachers are expected to undertake greater responsibility for professional development in their schools. As in other three-tier systems, New Mexico's top level is optional for teachers.

The system is similar to the one Michigan is mulling and to Wisconsin's, launched 1½ years ago. But there is also a standout difference: New Mexico, where the state pays the lion's share of school costs, attached a minimum-salary level to each classification. Provisional teachers must make at least $30,000, "professional" teachers at least $40,000, and "master" teachers, $50,000.

New Mexico officials say the new system has helped with problems of supply and quality.

"We've basically eradicated those classes with nobody there and unlicensed teachers," said Eduardo Holguin, the chief legislative lobbyist for the National Education Association-New Mexico. Over the past six years, the proportion of teachers on licensing waivers has dropped from 10 percent to 1 percent, while the number of teachers overall has risen, according to a new report to the New Mexico legislature. In addition, the report says, the share of teachers staying through the first three years has improved, from about two-thirds to three-quarters.

Of the roughly 10 percent of teachers who have tried to change levels so far, passing rates on the dossiers for first-time aspirants are around 85 percent. The state is gathering data to look at the effect of the three-tier system on student performance.

Money Matters

A majority of other states do not have most of the responsibility for salaries, and licensing-system effects will have to be achieved, if at all, without money attached.

Iowa's experience shows just how much funding counts. In 2001, the legislature passed a bill specifying a new licensing system that, with four levels, matched pay to four rungs of a so-called career ladder. Another change required new teachers to pass a classroom evaluation within two years to progress to a standard license. Neophytes also had to be enrolled locally in a state-approved mentoring program.

Moreover, the state required that holders of a standard license develop, with their evaluators, individualized professional goals and a plan to meet them. On that rested license renewal.

Before those changes, "licensing had not been tied in any way to evaluation of the job" the teacher was doing, said Judy A. Jeffrey, Iowa's schools chief.

Those provisions are in effect, but a sharp economic downturn doomed other parts of the system. Under the original plan, for instance, teachers were to get an increase of $10,000 to move from level 2 to level 3. The plan is still on the books, but no work is being done to flesh out the upper two levels of licensure, Ms. Jeffrey said.

One way states have connected pay and licensing is to add a third tier just for teachers who have achieved advanced certification through the national board. In most states, teachers with the credential receive additional pay. In Delaware, Illinois, and Kansas, they go up a notch in licensing, too.

Wisconsin's three-tier system, now in its second year, accepts national certification for its "master" level, or candidates can hold a master's degree and go through a similar assessment graded by a state-trained team of educators.

"I think it's the best thing we've done in a long time in regard to licensing," said Jim Carlson, a negotiator for local NEA unions in the Sheboygan, Wis., area. "It offers a vision of a future for a young teacher, and they are more likely to stay in the business because of it."

Since Wisconsin teachers move up through providing evidence of their skills, such as videotapes of teaching, licensing is related to classroom endeavors in ways that simply completing courses or workshops is not, he added. Plus, the licensing structure offers district and union officials alike the opportunity to reorient pay scales around such performance.

'Ad Hoc' Development

Teacher experts don't dislike such licensing reforms, but they leave much undone, they say.

Kate Walsh, the president of the National Council on Teacher Quality, a Washington-based research and advocacy group, pointed out that no existing licensing system assesses teachers with a primary focus on student learning. Nor is that likely to happen until systems are in place that are able to measure a teacher's contribution to learning over a number of years, she said.

Linda Darling-Hammond, a Stanford University professor, countered that evaluation methods are much improved over 15 years ago even without that component.

Still, she said, other countries are "very far ahead" of the United States in fostering and recognizing teacher development. "If you look across [our] whole nation," Ms. Darling-Hammond said, "it is very ad hoc."

. . .

★ THE QUESTION OF PERFORMANCE PAY ★

**COMMENTARY BY JAMES W. GUTHRIE
AND PATRICK J. SCHUERMANN**
October 29, 2008

ALMOST THREE YEARS AGO, as many pay-for-performance initiatives for educators were in their formative stages and advocates were intensifying their campaign for expansion, we warned against moving forward faddishly, or mindlessly mimicking the mistakes associated with 1980s-style merit pay. ("Teacher Pay for Performance: Another Fad or a Sound and Lasting Policy?" *Commentary*, April 5, 2006.) We endorsed a gradual, incremental development of such compensation plans' design, and urged rigorous independent experimentation and objective evaluation.

In the intervening years, growth in this area of education policy has been anything but incremental. Performance pay has become a wildly popular option, and appears to be poised for even more dramatic future expansion.

There are now widespread federal, state, and local initiatives, along with foundation endorsements, technical support, and financial inducements (more than $500 million allocated for the 2008–09 school year) to expand incentive pay. States as diverse as Florida, Minnesota, South Dakota, Tennessee, and Texas have enacted statewide policies promoting performance pay for educators. National performance-pay models, such as the Milken Family Foundation's Teacher Advancement Program, or TAP, continue to expand, while creative district models have further evolved, including Denver's widely publicized ProComp plan. New models also are emerging, such as New York City's "schoolwide performance bonus program" supported by the United Federation of Teachers and the New York City Department of Education.

In some form or fashion, performance pay exists in approximately 10 percent of the nation's school districts and affects at least 20 percent of K–12 teachers and students. Its expansion continues despite the sour aftertaste left from the failed incentive-pay experiences of the 1980s—and perhaps in some part because of steadily increasing media attention.

Those who already are engaged in the operation of such plans, or are considering their adoption, should understand that there is still only the slenderest research base undergirding the effort. As yet, there are no rigorous empirical validations to show that U.S. performance-pay programs in education are linked to substantial and sustained successes, either in elevating student achievement or in accelerating the occupational attractiveness of education for a wider pool of able teacher candidates. In effect, while policy-system enthusiasm for the idea is building, the research-and-evaluation jury is still out on educator performance pay.

Even so, lessons can be learned from recent research results. These early findings and preliminary practical observations may provide little in the way of specifying a perfect performance-pay model, but they do suggest several important considerations in the design and implementation of such plans—as well as pitfalls to be avoided. Here is a brief summary of the knowns and unknowns about teacher performance pay, and what this knowledge may mean for future development of the concept.

What we know with a high degree of certainty:

- An effective teacher can contribute substantially to student achievement, regardless of students' innate abilities and home and neighborhood socioeconomic circumstances.

- Sustained, multiyear contact with an effective teacher can materially mitigate students' accumulated achievement deficits.

- Currently, the distribution of identified effective teachers favors students from higher socioeconomic circumstances.

- While current considerations in the determination of public school teacher pay—seniority and added academic credits—have ameliorated past injustices and provided predictability and objectivity, they display only minimal relationships with elevated student academic achievement.

What we suspect is true from experience and observation, but do not now know with certainty:

- Rewards hold the prospect of strongly shaping the effort of employees. But there is a possibility of dysfunctional goal-displacement—working hard on the highly rewarded goals but slighting others equally important. Consequently, architects of performance-pay plans must make sure that the conditions being measured and rewarded (accurately and comprehensively) reflect the organization's desired outcomes.

- Incentive-program designs almost always necessitate trade-offs between desirable qualities, such as transparency on the one hand and accuracy of performance measurement on the other. The increased complexity associated with accurately measuring teacher and school effectiveness, for example, often is associated with diminished transparency.

- Hastily conceived and overly simple plans often lead to mistakes and can engender low employee acceptance as a consequence. Hence, given the complexity of performance-award programs, it is important to initiate evaluative procedures and anticipate midcourse corrections from the outset.

- Three obstacles on which contemporary performance-pay programs appear most frequently to founder are (1) inaccurate, incomplete, or unfair measurements of student achievement and other outcomes; (2) unclear or insufficient efforts to explain the program to important stakeholders and gain their commitment; and (3) inaccurate projections of possible financial exposure and a consequent inability to pay as promised or sustain funding for the program.

What we do not yet know:

- The power of financial awards in promoting more-effective teaching and elevating student performance.

- The effects of group awards relative to individual performance awards.

- The preferable mix of financial and nonpecuniary awards.

- The long-term effect of performance awards on the supply of effective teachers.

- The consequences of offering higher pay for teachers in subject shortage areas and hard-to-staff schools.

- The cost-effectiveness of performance incentives relative to alternative strategies for elevating academic achievement, such as class-size reduction, enhanced reliance on educational specialists, or intensified deployment of technology.

In light of these conditions, our message to educators and policymakers remains much the same as it was three years ago: a cautious endorsement of careful performance-pay-plan design and a strong plea for rigorous independent experimentation and objective evaluation. What may be needed most is the kind of pragmatic experimentation advocated by Jack V. Matson, an environmental engineer, in his 1996 book *Innovate or Die*. Matson recommends, as one element of innovation, an analytical process for eliminating unsuitable design options that he terms "intelligent fast failure."

Intelligent fast failure is not a goal, but an outcome from risking effort. Each experiment undertaken is carefully considered, with the goal being to determine the conditions necessary for success. Experiments are crafted to minimize downside risks and the time and resources needed to learn quickly from the outcomes. While ordinarily one would test ideas sequentially, starting with the best, with intelligent fast failure an institution experiments with multiple ideas simultaneously. As a result, it is possible to accelerate the learning process, compress failure time, and progress more rapidly toward resolution.

With today's proliferation of performance-pay plans, it is important that educators systematically collect, document, and share widely what is being learned from such programs. Lessons passed on by practitioners and researchers represent assets of tremendous value to states and districts interested in designing and implementing performance-pay plans of their own. Similarly, empirically based assessments of the short- and long-term consequences of performance pay will allow both the policy and practitioner communities to move forward with greater certainty.

By harvesting contextually rich insights based on research, and by harnessing the potential of processes such as intelligent fast failure, we can move the performance-pay phenomenon further from being a passing fad and closer to being a sound and lasting policy.

. . .

★ SEEKING — AND FINDING — ★
GOOD TEACHING

COMMENTARY BY JULIE SWEETLAND
October 22, 2008

EDUCATION POLICYMAKERS are starting to act on what teachers have long known: No matter what policies, curricula, or governance structures are in place, they are only as effective as the teacher who translates them into the daily life of the classroom. Issues of teacher quality are absolutely critical, because research shows that teachers are the single most influential school-based factor in student success. As the education establishment increases its focus on excellent instruction, it's imperative that the players in the teacher-quality arena don't take the politically expedient but educationally dangerous shortcut of equating good teaching with high student test scores.

If the goal is to foster excellent teaching, a better alternative may be to finally invest in a dramatically improved approach to teacher evaluation. It's time to adopt an approach that creates a common language of what good teaching looks like, helps everyone in a school system learn that language, and provides a clear means of supporting them as they walk the talk.

The task is difficult, but the time is right. There are signs that the standards movement that has dominated public discussion on school reform for the past decade is finally giving way to a teacher-quality movement. At every level of governance, a consensus is emerging that teacher-quality policies are something that we have to get right. Both major-party candidates in the presidential race are tackling the issue of performance pay for educators. On Capitol Hill, a Democratic plan for revising the federal No Child Left Behind Act includes devoting major federal funding to research into performance assessments for teachers. In the high-profile local school reform effort under way in the nation's capital, schools Chancellor Michelle Rhee is looking for ways to link teacher effectiveness to compensation. In this, the District of Columbia school system would be following in the footsteps of districts such as Denver, Minneapolis, and Toledo, Ohio—all of which have adopted innovative approaches to improving teacher evaluations.

Since supporting effective instruction is the school reform that matters most for student achievement, districts placing a high priority on direct observations of classroom practice appear to be on the right track. In Toledo, for example, teachers become eligible for performance bonuses based on a multiple-method evaluation that includes peer ratings, up to six classroom observations, assessment of written-communication skills, and a standards-based portfolio. Another mixed-methods approach is the Teacher Advancement Program, or TAP, which is being implemented in more than 200 schools nationwide. In many of the TAP schools, teachers can earn bonuses based on a combination of schoolwide test scores and five classroom evaluations performed by trained observers.

The observations used in these systems are far from the hastily scribbled, ill-defined checklists that are the most common form of teacher evaluations—and which often aren't really evaluations at all, but instead are a tedious chore that neither administrators nor teachers enjoy, value, or trust. Rigorous classroom evaluations aren't just someone's opinion; they are carefully conducted qualitative assessments that meet research standards for clarity and transparency. They guide trained observers to look for specific indicators of excellent instruction: effective questioning that pushes students to think critically; the ability to foster a positive, productive classroom environment; the use of engaging lessons that draw students into the learning process.

These are among the indicators of great instruction that cut across teaching situations—they're applicable in every grade, in every subject, in every school. Far from being a "warm and fuzzy" approach to teacher evaluation that merely distracts from the "real" issue of student achievement, substantive teacher-performance assessments focus on nationally recognized standards for quality teaching. And where there is quality teaching, there is student learning.

The idea of direct performance assessments for teachers isn't new. It just hasn't been done widely, or well, because it takes more money and more expertise than cheaper, easier alternatives such as the "drive by" principal evaluations that are ubiquitous in most public school systems. But by not paying upfront for meaningful and fair teacher evaluation, we pay later in costs to the profession. Effective teachers never get the recognition they deserve, and they leave the profession at higher rates than their less effective peers; schools have no way to hold underperforming teachers accountable, short of firing them; and the teachers in the middle rarely receive the type of constructive feedback that could inspire them to refine their craft.

By not paying upfront for meaningful and fair teacher evaluation, we pay later in costs to the profession.

The glaring inadequacies in low-stakes, low-quality administrator evaluations are one factor that has added to the popularity of using student test scores as a more reliable alternative. It's unclear, however, that replacing quick-and-dirty classroom observations with quick-and-dirty test scores represents progress toward the goal of collecting reliable data that would help all concerned recognize and foster excellent teaching. The problem with using achievement tests for teacher evaluations is that they simply aren't designed for that purpose, and so they are too blunt an instrument.

Instructional leaders who have been hip-deep in test data for years have already found that reading and math scores alone don't offer the level of detail they need to make wise decisions about teacher professional development. For that, they typically rely on what they've seen in the classroom. Why? While test results allow only for a discussion of the "what" of student achievement, looking directly at classroom instruction can tell teachers and administrators the "why" and "how." With a substantive assessment of which aspects of instruction are working and which aren't, teachers can be more purposefully directed on the path to excellence.

Although proponents of standardized tests argue that they are the most practical method of getting reliable data, there are significant logistical roadblocks to using them for measuring teacher effectiveness. The biggest is that fewer than half the teachers in any school district teach a tested grade or subject, which begs the question of what the increasingly popular "value added" approach will do with the Spanish teacher, the history teacher, or the kindergarten teacher.

Worse, linking high-stakes employment decisions to children's performance on a single test could create a truly dangerous dynamic in classrooms. We've already seen the unintended but depressing effects of the testing craze on a national scale: Art, music, and even recess are being abandoned in an effort to make more time for test prep. Increasing the pressure by upping the stakes will only increase the negative backlash. A struggling child threatens the bottom line on a bonus check; a high-scoring child becomes the goose that will lay the golden egg. Students could retaliate against an unpopular teacher by collectively bombing a test. The temptation to fudge the numbers would certainly increase.

If what we really want is quality teaching,
shouldn't we take the time to look for it?

As the national and local debates over teacher merit pay continue, decisionmakers should instead support evaluation measures that recognize and reward teachers who create rich, rigorous, and relevant learning experiences for children. Tests simply can't capture the information we need. If what we really want is quality teaching, shouldn't we take the time to look for it?

. . .

★ TEACHING AT THE PRECIPICE ★

Strengthening Teacher Retention and
Recruitment for the Long Haul

COMMENTARY BY ARTHUR E. LEVINE

AND DAVID HASELKORN

November 5, 2008

WITH NEARLY HALF of all new teachers leaving their classrooms within five years and as many as a third of the nation's teaching force readying for retirement, some education and political leaders seem to believe that education can solve its human-resource challenge by becoming more like the military: sign individuals up for short-term enlistments, prepare them in intensive boot-camp experiences, and then send them to the front lines.

As with the armed forces (or even higher education), the answer, these leaders propose, is to supply sufficient teachers by supplementing a small, permanent staff with a large corps of short-timers.

The situation reminds us of the Yiddish tale of the wise men of Chelm.

Chelm, an Eastern European shtetl not known for its brilliance, lay at the base of a cliff. After dark, wandering travelers sometimes fell off the cliff and landed, badly hurt, in the middle of Chelm. Following a rash of such injuries, the shtetl's governing group, its wise men, convened to find a solution to this problem. They deliberated intensely for three days and three nights, then announced their solemn determination: They would build a hospital at the bottom of the cliff.

Rather than preventing injuries to travelers, the wise men of Chelm chose to treat the injured. They accepted the problem as immutable.

Rebuilding the teaching profession around current attrition patterns is a lot like building a hospital at the bottom of the cliff—shortsighted and ultimately counterproductive. Instead, we need to provide teachers with solid preparation and support that will help keep them in the classroom.

Study after study has shown that experienced teachers are more effective in raising student academic performance. Research conducted by the Education Schools Project, for example, found student achievement in math and reading significantly higher in classes taught by teachers with 10 years of experience, compared with those taught by peers with less than five years on the job. Over 12 years of schooling, the differential is nearly a year's achievement in math and more than a year in reading.

We can help retain teachers by ameliorating the key problems that cause them to leave: poor salaries, bad working conditions, low status, and too little preparation for the classroom.

States and school districts can raise teacher salaries, which are low compared to that of the average college graduate with a comparable degree, and the disparity grows the longer a teacher remains in the classroom. They can also provide higher pay for teachers working in hard-to-staff schools or high-need fields.

Districts can improve working conditions by placing talented principals in schools and appointing district leaders committed to turning teaching into a career ladder. With differentiated opportunities and responsibilities throughout their careers, as well as ongoing professional development, teachers can move up this ladder.

Teachers' unions can assist by treating their members as professionals rather than craft workers. This requires real courage and leadership from unions and genuine commitment from communities, school boards, and superintendents to make the arrangement a true quid pro quo for teachers. As Denver's re-ratification of its ProComp pay-for-performance plan has once again proved, teachers will accept greater responsibility for their efforts to raise achievement in exchange for higher pay, fair evaluation (including peer review), and more meaningful professional development.

In hard fiscal times, such proposals may sound costly. But in the long run, investments that improve teacher retention will cost less than revolving-door recruitment. The National Commission on Teaching and America's Future has estimated the cost of replacing teachers who turn over in the early years at $15,000 to $20,000 per teacher in our largest urban schools. The additional cost of re-mediation for students who lack expert teachers more than doubles that amount.

An emerging body of research suggests both that better-prepared teachers are more effective as first-year teachers, and that teachers who are more effective stay in teaching longer. (See studies by the New York Pathways to Teaching project and work by John M. Krieg, Eric A. Hanushek, Dan Goldhaber, and Kimberly Barraza Lyons, for example.)

Along with better initial preparation, two to three years of teacher mentoring and induction must become the norm. During this time, novice teachers would undergo an arc of professional growth comparable to those of medical residencies and legal training, where developing knowledge and skill is closely monitored and supported.

To ensure that teachers have more effective leaders helping them improve their work, we should develop a national system of board certification for school principals, akin to that undertaken by the growing cadre of teachers certified by the National Board for Professional Teaching Standards, who are demonstrating their effectiveness in the classroom.

All this would go a long way toward ensuring that all students have good teachers, but states and districts also need to be more aggressive in recruiting—and more innovative in preparing—a broader talent pool for teaching. Better salaries and support can make teaching more attractive to recent graduates with strong academic credentials.

Potential career-changers also should be more creatively and aggressively recruited to teach. A Peter Hart survey done for our group, the Woodrow Wilson National Fellowship Foundation, found that two of every five college-educated Americans between the ages of 24 and 60—almost 20 million adults—would consider switching to a teaching career given the right conditions and compensation. These potential teachers are likelier than others to have a postgraduate degree, to have attended selective colleges, and to report having higher-than-average grades. They are also likelier to stay in the field longer, because many want a long-term career change that is more personally rewarding and more compatible with family responsibilities than previous jobs.

What would it take to get more of them to switch? Findings show that starting salaries in the $50,000 range—just $10,000 to $15,000 above many districts' current starting salary—could do it, along with well-tailored, high-quality training and support.

The real challenge will be paying for this. Gary K. Hart, California's former secretary of education, has suggested that state boards of education be authorized to certify critical-need areas, such as high school science and math, special education, or low-performing schools. States and participating local school districts could then each provide a $5,000 salary augmentation to new teachers who come to these fields with valuable expertise from other careers. They could fund such supplements by eliminating or reducing lower-priority programs and identifying willing corporate and foundation partners.

Some leaders propose alternative pay systems that would provide more money upfront for new teachers and faster pay increases for those who have proved themselves in the classroom. This approach would also help keep more teachers on the job during the years when they are forming families or paying off student loans, and when they are most likely to be lured away to other positions.

The point is, we need and can develop equitable, attractive alternatives to crash-course teacher preparation, the current salary-step system, and the revolving-door approach. We *must* do so to encourage both persistence and performance and to recruit a larger supply of qualified teachers.

Rebuilding the teaching profession calls for an emphasis on building teacher capacity and longevity in the classroom. On the precipice of major demographic change, as many districts face growing enrollments and a chasm created by retirements, states and school districts must think in new ways about retention and recruitment. When good teachers stay in the profession longer, students perform better and school districts save money. When we tap in to the large pool of college-educated adults who might teach, we can address teaching's most critical staffing needs. And we can do it without resorting to building hospitals at the bottom of cliffs. We cannot afford to miss—or give up on—the problem.

. . .

★ A MARSHALL PLAN FOR TEACHING ★

What It Will Really Take to Leave No Child Behind

ADAPTED FROM COMMENTARY BY LINDA DARLING-HAMMOND

January 10, 2007

VIEWS ABOUT the No Child Left Behind Act are currently as divided as Berlin before the wall came down. But whatever one thinks about the act, it's clear that developing more-skillful teaching is a sine qua non for attaining higher and more equitable achievement for students in the United States. Without teachers who have sophisticated skills for teaching challenging content to diverse learners, there is no way that children from all racial and ethnic, language, and socioeconomic backgrounds will reach the high academic standards envisioned by the law. For this reason, one of the most important aspects of the No Child Left Behind legislation is its demand for a "highly qualified" teacher for every child.

Research indicates that expert teachers are the most important—and the most inequitably distributed—school resource. In the United States, however, schools serving more than 1 million of our highest-need students are staffed by a parade of underprepared and inexperienced teachers who know little about effective instruction, and even less about teaching English-language learners and students with disabilities. Many of these teachers enter the classroom with little training and leave soon after, creating greater instability in their wake. Meanwhile, affluent students receive teachers who are typically better prepared than their predecessors, further widening the achievement gap.

This constant attrition of underprepared teachers creates a harmful cycle in which students are constantly learning from inexperienced and less-effective teachers. This undermines achievement and costs the nation billions of dollars in wasted resources. Estimates of the costs of beginning-teacher attrition average about $15,000 to $20,000 for each teacher who leaves, money that could have been more productively spent on training and mentoring that would improve teacher effectiveness and retention.

Research indicates that expert teachers are the most important— and the most inequitably distributed—school resource.

This is not smart policy. The notion that we can remain a world-class economy while undereducating large portions of our population—in particular, students of color and new immigrants, who are fast becoming a majority in our public schools—is untenable. Mostly because of these underinvestments, the United States continues to rank far behind other industrialized nations in educational achievement: 28th out of 40 nations in mathematics in 2003, for example, right behind Latvia. Meanwhile, leaders of countries like Finland that experienced a meteoric rise to the top of the international rankings have attributed their success to their massive investments in teacher education.

Most of the higher-achieving countries we consider peers or competitors now provide high-quality graduate-level teacher education designed to ensure that teachers can effectively educate all of their students. Preparation is usually fully subsidized for all entrants, and includes a year of practice teaching in a clinical school connected to the university. Schools receive funding to provide coaching, seminars, classroom visits, and joint planning time for beginners as well as veterans. Salaries are competitive with those in other professions and include additional stipends for hard-to-staff locations.

If we are serious about leaving no child behind, we need to go beyond mandates to ensure that *all* students have well-qualified teachers. Effective action can be modeled after practices in medicine. Since 1944, the federal government has subsidized medical training to fill shortages and build teaching hospitals and training programs in high-need areas—a commitment that has contributed significantly to America's world-renowned system of medical training and care.

Intelligent, targeted incentives can ensure that all students have access to teachers who are indeed highly qualified. An aggressive national policy on teacher quality and supply, on the order of the post-World War II Marshall Plan, could be accomplished for less than 1 percent of the more than $300 billion spent thus far in Iraq, and, in a matter of only a few years, would establish a world-class teaching force in all communities.

• First, the federal government should establish *service scholarships* to cover training costs in high-quality programs at the undergraduate and graduate levels for young and midcareer recruits who will teach in high-need fields or locations for at least four years. (After three years, teachers are more likely to remain in the profession and make a difference for student achievement.) Because fully prepared novices are twice as likely to stay in teaching as those who lack training, shortages could be reduced rapidly if districts could hire better-prepared teachers. Virtually all the vacancies currently filled with emergency teachers could be filled with well-prepared teachers if 40,000 service scholarships of up to $25,000 each were offered annually. (Price tag: $1 billion per year.)

• Second, *recruitment incentives* are needed to attract and retain expert, experienced teachers in high-need schools. Federal matching grants could leverage additional compensation for teachers with expertise and/or additional responsibilities, such as mentoring or coaching. If matched by state or local contributions, stipends of $10,000 for 50,000 teachers annually—based on systems that recognize teacher expertise, such as National Board for Professional Teaching Standards certification, standards-based evaluations, and carefully assembled evidence of contributions to student learning—could attract 100,000 accomplished teachers to high-poverty schools to serve as mentors and master teachers. An additional $300 million in matching grants could be used toward improved teaching conditions in these schools, including smaller pupil loads, adequate materials, and time for teacher planning and professional development—all of which keep teachers in schools. (Price tag: $800 million a year.)

• Third, as is true in medicine, the Marshall Plan for Teaching should support *improved preparation.* Incentive grants ($300 million annually) should upgrade all teachers' preparation for teaching literacy skills as well as standards-based content, and for teaching special education students and English-language learners. An additional $200 million per year should be used to expand state-of-the-art teacher education programs in high-need communities that partner "teaching schools" with universities. As in teaching hospitals, candidates in these schools study teaching and learning while gaining hands-on experience in state-of-the-art classrooms. Effective models have already been created by universities sponsoring professional-development schools and by school districts offering urban teacher residencies that place candidates with expert teachers while they complete their coursework. These programs create a pipeline of teachers prepared to engage in best practice, while establishing demonstration sites for urban teaching. Funding for 200 programs serving an average of 150 candidates each, at $1 million per year per program, would supply 30,000 exceptionally well-prepared recruits to high-need communities each year. (Price tag: $500 million per year.)

• Fourth, providing *mentoring for all beginning teachers* would reduce attrition and increase competence. With one-third of new teachers leaving the classroom within five years, and higher rates of attrition for those who are underprepared, recruitment efforts are like pouring water into a leaky bucket. By investing in state and district induction programs, we could ensure mentoring support for every new teacher in the nation. Based on the funding model used in California's successful Beginning Teacher Support and Assessment program, a federal allocation of $4,000 for each of 125,000 beginning teachers, matched by states or local districts, could ensure that each novice is coached by a trained mentor. (Price tag: $500 million a year.)

• Finally, preparation and mentoring can be strengthened if they are guided by a high-quality *teacher-performance assessment* that measures actual teaching skill. Current tests used for licensing and federal accountability are typically paper-and-pencil measures of basic skills and subject-matter knowledge that demonstrate little about teachers' abilities to practice effectively. Performance assessments for new teachers in states like Connecticut and California have been strong levers for improving preparation and mentoring, and for determining teachers' competence. Federal support to develop a nationally available performance assessment for licensing would not only provide a useful tool for accountability and improvement, but would also help teachers move more easily from states with surpluses to those with shortages. (Price tag: $100 million per year.)

In the long run, these proposals would save far more than they cost. The savings would include the more than $2 billion now wasted annually because of high teacher turnover, plus the even higher costs of grade retention, summer school, remedial programs, lost wages, and prison sentences for dropouts (another $50 billion, increasingly tied to illiteracy and school failure). A Marshall Plan for Teaching could help ensure that the United States, within only a few years, could place well-qualified teachers in the schools that most need them and give all students a genuine opportunity to learn.

CHAPTER 8

Improve College Access and Affordability

"Every American has the right to pursue their dreams. But we also have the responsibility to make sure that our children can reach a little further and rise a little higher than we did."

BARACK OBAMA

Bettendorf, Iowa, November 7, 2007

THE ISSUE

To be successful in the 21st century economy, America's workforce must be more innovative and productive than our competitors. Giving every American the opportunity to attend and afford and be successful in college is critical to meeting that challenge. As tuition costs swell and grant-aid fails to keep pace, students and their families are having a harder time paying for college.

These trends not only threaten our competitiveness in the global marketplace, but also our ability to maintain and improve our economy at home. Barack Obama and Joe Biden want to reverse these trends by making sure that a college education is affordable and within reach of every American.

THE OBAMA PLAN

The Obama-Biden plan includes proposals to:

- **Support College Outreach Programs:** Support outreach programs like GEAR UP, TRIO, and Upward Bound to encourage more young people from low-income families to consider and prepare for college.

- **Support College Credit Initiatives:** Create a national "Make College A Reality" initiative that has a bold goal to increase students taking AP or college-level classes nationwide 50 percent by 2016, and will build on Obama's bipartisan proposal in the U.S. Senate to provide grants for students seeking college level credit at community colleges if their school does not provide those resources.

- **Create the American Opportunity Tax Credit:** Make college affordable for all Americans by creating a new American Opportunity Tax Credit. This universal and fully refundable credit will ensure that the first $4,000 of a college education is completely free for most Americans, and will cover two-thirds the cost of tuition at the average public college or university and make community college tuition completely free for most students. Recipients of the credit will be required to conduct 100 hours of community service.

- **Simplify the Application Process for Financial Aid:** Streamline the financial aid process by eliminating the current federal financial aid application and enabling families to apply simply by checking a box on their tax form, authorizing their tax information to be used, and eliminating the need for a separate application.

. . .

DISTRICT FOCUSES ON PATHWAYS TO COLLEGE

BY CHRISTINA A. SAMUELS
June 11, 2008

MANY HIGH SCHOOL SENIORS have great plans to attend college after they graduate. All too often, those plans outstrip reality.

Some find out that they do not have the academic foundation to be candidates for college. Others are held back by complicated financial-aid applications, difficulties writing an entrance essay, or an overreliance on one college choice that may ultimately fall through.

The 409,000-student Chicago school district has taken a comprehensive approach to try to remove as many roadblocks as possible from the paths of high school students, through its 5-year-old department of postsecondary education and student development.

Where They Go

Though many states and districts are rallying around the idea of creating a seamless transition from high school to college, Chicago is considered at the forefront of such efforts.

"Nobody is doing the type of work that is going on in Chicago," said Ann S. Coles, the senior adviser for college-access programs for the Education Resources Institute Inc., a nonprofit guarantor of student loans in Boston. Her organization is also the directing partner of the Pathways to College Network, a coalition of education groups working to improve college access and success for underrepresented students.

Arne Duncan, the chief executive officer of the district, also believes Chicago's efforts are ambitious. "Just having students graduate from high school can't be our goal," he said. "We're working to change the culture of expectations."

Since the creation of the department, the Chicago system has seen its college-attendance rate edge up from 43.5 percent for the class of 2004 to 50 percent for the class of 2007.

Accurate Numbers

Using statistics culled from local sources and from national sources like the National Student Clearinghouse, the department seeks first to get a clear idea of where students are ending up. Before educators had such sources of hard information, said the department's director, Gregory M. Darnieder, the estimates that school officials would give of college-attendance rates tended to be too rosy.

"Their estimates are typically 20 to 30 percentage points higher than the reality was," he said.

The department has deployed "postsecondary coaches" in high schools to work with students and guidance counselors on students' college readiness. Each coach reports to a postsecondary specialist, who works with many high schools.

To make sure that those who are college-ready don't fall by the wayside because they lack the money, the postsecondary department worked with the Illinois Student Assistance Commission to track students' completion of the Free Application for Federal Student Aid, or FAFSA. The FAFSA is the information that most colleges use to determine student need and to craft financial-aid packages.

Failing to fill out the form, or filling it out incorrectly, can derail some students' college-attendance plans.

The district has also promoted more-traditional college-readiness efforts. This school year, for the first time, it hosted a spring-break college tour that drew 500 students. And the post-secondary department has overseen the local rollout of a national college-readiness program for elementary, middle, and high school students called Advancement Via Individual Determination, or AVID, which provides students academic support and teaches college-going strategies.

"This is all about creating a school culture where college is a possible goal," Mr. Darnieder said.

Tracking Data

The district's efforts are supported by the Consortium on Chicago School Research, based at the University of Chicago. Jenny K. Nagaoka, the project director for the postsecondary-transition project at the consortium, said her group and the district are analyzing the same data. The consortium's role, she said, is to give the district an idea of which statistics, out of the stacks of data available, make the most difference in getting students to enroll in college.

"Otherwise, it's just random pieces of information," Ms. Nagaoka said.

The focus on the FAFSA is one example. The consortium released a report in March called "From High School to the Future: Potholes on the Way to College." Researchers, including Ms. Nagaoka, a report co-author, interviewed 105 Chicago high school students and discovered that although 72 percent aspired to enter a four-year college, financial-aid applications were a significant barrier for some, particularly Latino students.

Other barriers were applying to only one school. Now, the district encourages students to apply to a number of schools, Ms. Nagaoka said.

The findings were shared with the district in 2006, to give it time to work on the issues raised, she said.

Francisco J. Rios, a postsecondary coach based at the district's 2,000-student Hubbard High School, said the school once appeared to devote most of its attention to a handful of top students who were considered college material. Many students outside the top tier felt that college wasn't a realistic option, he noted.

"When I first started at Hubbard, not too many came to actually talk to me about college," Mr. Rios said. "The other kids thought, 'Well, I'm in the middle, why should I even try?'"

That mind-set has changed over time, he said. One important goal now is to work with parents, who sometimes don't know what financial aid is available for their children. Once parents learn about scholarships and other aid, they see the opportunities available, Mr. Rios said.

Chicago's efforts to use data to guide its work in high schools is notable, said Bruce Vandal, the director of the postsecondary education and workforce-development institute at the Denver-based Education Commission of the States. Aligning data systems so that districts can track students from preschool all the way through college is a "hot topic" at the moment, he said.

But such efforts have been complicated and time-consuming, and there's also the question of what schools should do with the information once they have it. "That's the huge part," Mr. Vandal said. "How do they use that data to reform what they do at the high schools?"

One challenge has been incorporating the work of the coaches, based at each school, with guidance counselors, said Eric Z. Williams, a postsecondary specialist who oversees coaches at 22 schools. Some of the work done by coaches has traditionally been conducted by guidance counselors.

"We're still sorting all of that out," he said. "Certainly we see the coaches as complementary, equal co-workers in serving the students and serving the schools."

The sense among officials is that the department is succeeding. Mayor Richard M. Daley earlier last month lauded the college-enrollment-rate numbers for the class of 2007. "The conversations in all of our high schools across the city are changing from 'How do I get to graduation day?' to 'Where is the best place for me to continue my education?'" the mayor said.

. . .

COLLEGE-COST 'EMERGENCY' JEOPARDIZES ACCESS

BY SCOTT J. CECH
December 3, 2008

HIT BY THE DOUBLE WHAMMY of soaring tuition and stagnant wages, too many Americans are seeing college slipping out of their grasp, warns the head of a biennial report card on postsecondary education that was released today.

Comparing the dramatic rise in college costs with global warming, Patrick M. Callan, the president of the National Center for Public Policy and Higher Education, is calling for a new kind of social contract to address what he sees as an "emergency" in the affordability of higher education, as documented in his Washington-based nonprofit organization's fifth comprehensive report on the state of higher education.

Mr. Callan cited data from the report showing that the cost of college tuition and fees soared 439 percent between the early 1980s and 2006—almost double the 251 percent rise in medical costs over the same time. He also underscored the finding that middle- and upper-income students receive larger grants from colleges than low-income students do.

The result, he said, could be a decline in the proportion of people going to college. "If we don't begin to act on that now, we could see an absolute decline," he said in a phone conference with reporters ahead of the report's release. "When the ice cap has melted, . . . it's too late to fix it."

Flunking the Affordability Test

The report, "Measuring Up 2008," gave every state an F on college affordability except California, which received a C, mostly because its community colleges are so inexpensive.

Mr. Callan said the affordability problem is compounded by the failure of federal grants to keep up with costs, and a higher-education-financing system that he called "a political football."

"By and large, tuition is not policy-driven in the states," he said. During more prosperous times when students can afford to pay a little more, tuition is often frozen or only slightly raised, Mr. Callan said. "And then, when the economy is bad," he added, "we sock it to the students." That cycle occurs in part because state higher education budgets are also often cut during recessions such as the current one, he said.

Mr. Callan called for "a new social contract" that would allow the parents of a 6-year-old child to more accurately calculate how much they will need to save to pay for college a dozen years later. He also called for the elimination of "duplicative" graduate-level programs and the redirection of more faculty time toward educating undergraduates.

Tony Pals, a spokesman for the National Association of Independent Colleges and Universities, a Washington-based organization of more than 900 private institutions, said his group's members have worked hard to make higher education more affordable.

"Especially in light of the credit crunch and economic turmoil, it's critical for all parties to work together to fulfill the promise of educational opportunity for people of all backgrounds," he said in an e-mail.

"Private college and university presidents are committed to thinking and acting creatively to enhance their affordability, within their institutions' financial means," Mr. Pals said. "In the past 10 years, institutionally provided grant aid at private colleges has grown by 250 percent, compared to a 72 percent increase in published tuition."

When adjusted for inflation, he said, the increase in tuition and fees over the past five years at private colleges is at its lowest level since 1982.

K–12 Preparation Up

Compared with affordability, states got better grades in the report on K–12 academic preparation, including high school completion, the rigor of math and science courses taken, student proficiency, and teacher quality. Six states—Colorado, Connecticut, Maryland, Massachusetts, New Jersey, and Vermont—received A's, most states got B's or C's, and only five states got D's. There were no F's in the K–12-preparation category in this year's report, unlike the 2006 "Measuring Up" report, which gave F's to Louisiana and New Mexico.

But Joni E. Finney, the vice president of the San Jose, Calif.-based center and the principal author of the state reports, noted that better K–12 preparation wasn't being matched by college enrollments.

"We're not seeing the enrollment that we should see, given the improvement in preparation over time," said Ms. Finney, who is also a professor at the University of Pennsylvania's graduate school of education.

Mr. Callan attributed that gap to the erosion of affordability.

"We have a lot of people whose college aspirations are fragile," he said. Those people include adults who would be the first in their families to attend college, but who must balance the future opportunities presented by higher education against costs and the need to work, he said.

If colleges cut back on needed classes, Mr. Callan said, it doesn't matter how academically well prepared students are: "They don't hang around and wait for the budget to come back."

· · ·

PANEL PROPOSES MAJOR OVERHAUL OF COLLEGE-AID SYSTEM

BY SCOTT J. CECH

September 24, 2008

A HIGH-PROFILE NATIONAL PANEL of experts convened by the New York City-based College Board last week issued a sweeping set of recommendations aimed at dramatically reconfiguring the way the roughly $86 billion in federal financial aid is delivered to U.S. college students every year.

Under one of the panel's proposals, the repayment of student loans would be based on post-college financial circumstances, and payment amounts would increase over time on the presumption that graduates' incomes would also rise.

The federal application form for student aid would also be eliminated, in favor of information provided directly by the Internal Revenue Service; federal Pell Grant maximums would be linked to the Consumer Price Index; and federal Stafford loan amounts would be linked to the inflation-sensitive federal poverty level, if the panel's proposals were implemented.

"We need a student-aid system that is simple and clear and puts the money in the hands of those who need it," said Rethinking Student Aid study group co-chair Michael S. McPherson, the president of the Chicago-based Spencer Foundation, which helped underwrite the group's work.

Replace Subsidies

The panel of professors and foundation officials cited cost estimates by the Washington-based Urban-Brookings Tax Policy Center suggesting that one of the proposals—replacing the federal subsidy of Stafford-loan interest payments while students are still in college with post-collegial payment adjustments based on financial circumstances—would save $8 billion per year.

The recommendations also include a federal savings plan for low-income families. Under the plan, the government would calculate how much Pell Grant money a child would be eligible for if he or she were of college age, based on his or her family's financial circumstances, and begin sending the family regular statements about how much money has been set aside so far for the child.

Patterned after the Social Security system, such accounts would involve no actual transfer of money until the child reached age 18. Rather, they would represent the federal government's financial commitment to pay the specified amount, which would accumulate tax-free interest, and be spendable only for college expenses.

"We need to make sure we get the message to low- and moderate-income families early that they're going to be able to pay for college," said Mr. McPherson. "We wanted to make aid not only simpler, but more predictable."

The cost of the proposals, group members said, would depend on how policymakers deployed them.

For example, one option would be for policymakers to base eligibility for the savings accounts on students' financial circumstances at age 12. Under that scenario, according to the group's projections, starting an annual savings deposit equal to 10 percent of the Pell Grant amount for which the child would be eligible would mean that over 12 million children would be served, at a cost of $2.8 billion per year at current college-participation rates.

David Hawkins, the director of public policy and research for the Alexandria, Va.-based National Association for College Admission Counseling, said such proposals have historically made little headway, but this time, the proposals' timing might be right.

Prospects Uncertain

"In light of the estimated $6 billion shortfall in the Pell Grant program, a student-loan market suffering from many of the same over-aggressive lending strategies as the mortgage market, and an economy that appears to be headed for rock bottom, it is possible that policymakers may be interested in ensuring that federal funds are spent efficiently and effectively to allow students the opportunity to attend college without incurring untenable debt," Mr. Hawkins said.

Robert M. Shireman, the president of the Berkeley, Calif.-based Institute for College Access and Success, said in an e-mail, "Too often these types of commissions produce unrealistic wish lists and vague exhortations. In contrast, this group took a more hardheaded, analytical approach. There are enough specifics so that policymakers could actually follow up."

Representatives of both Rep. George Miller, D-Calif., the House Education and Labor Committee chairman, and Rep. Howard P. "Buck" McKeon, R-Calif., its ranking minority member, said the congressmen welcomed the effort and would study the proposals.

Education Department spokeswoman Samara Yudof said U.S. Secretary of Education Margaret Spellings commended the group's work, and would continue to work toward simplifying the financial-aid system.

• • •

WHAT DOES 'READY' MEAN?

BY LYNN OLSON
June 12, 2007

AS HIGH SCHOOL COMMENCEMENT time rolls around, states are working to ensure that their graduates are "ready" for life after high school.

Eleven states report that they have adopted a definition of "college readiness," and 14 more are in the process of doing so. Twenty-one states report they have a definition of "work readiness," and 10 more states are tackling the issue.

Despite all the activity, there is still plenty of confusion about precisely what it means to be "college" or "career" ready. Do Americans expect all students to be ready for college *and* work—or just for one or the other? And if they're saying all students should be ready for both, does that mean every teenager must have exactly the same preparation in high school?

Do Americans expect all students to be ready for college and work—or just for one or the other?

A few things are clear, as an analysis conducted by the Editorial Projects in Education Research Center for this report shows: having at least some college under your belt is more likely to land you a decent job at a decent wage. And young people who lack a high school diploma have a tough time finding any job at all.

Because the discussion about college and career readiness typically tilts heavily toward preparation for college, this edition of *Diplomas Count* looks more closely at what it means to be "career ready," based on the recognition that even college graduates will eventually have to find their way in the labor market.

While better defining college and career readiness requires the formal involvement of both higher education and the business community, state K–12 players, in general, have found it easier to reach out to their postsecondary brethren than to employers. In part, that's because most states lack the business equivalent of a university system's board of regents. In addition, local businesses come in all shapes and sizes—making it hard to define the target job market for which high school graduates should be prepared.

"The task here is not to figure out what a student leaving high school needs to know in order to do any first job they're going to get when they leave high school," says Michael Cohen, the president of the Washington-based nonprofit group Achieve, which focuses on issues of college and workforce readiness. "There are plenty of those jobs that don't require high skills and that high schools shouldn't be expected to prepare students for, because they don't open doors of opportunity."

In contrast, he argues, states need to focus on areas of high-skill, high-wage job growth that may not necessarily require a four-year college degree, but typically do require some education and training beyond high school.

To help states see how large that job market is, the EPE Research Center has conducted an analysis for this report that examines the distribution of jobs within each state and the related education and pay levels.

Young people who lack a high school diploma
have a tough time finding any job at all.

The analysis uses information from the Occupational Information Network, or O*NET, a database developed for the U.S. Department of Labor. O*NET classifies jobs into five "zones," each defined by various worker attributes, including particular education, training, and experience requirements. Using another national database—the American Community Survey, conducted by the U.S. Census Bureau—the EPE Research Center is able to show what proportions of adults in each state hold occupations in the various job zones, their median earnings, and their average education levels.

The findings underscore that to earn a decent wage in this country, young people need to anticipate completing at least some college. For Job Zone 3, for which the median annual income is $35,672 nationally, 37 percent of jobholders have some college education and another 26 percent hold a bachelor's degree. For Job Zone 4, with a median annual income of $50,552, fully 68 percent of jobholders have a bachelor's degree and 21 percent have some college. Fewer than 1 in 10 employees in Job Zone 3 or higher have less than a high school diploma.

At the bottom end of the job-zone classifications, in which workers with a high school diploma or less are concentrated, the median annual income is $12,638 a year.

But while the analysis confirms the strong link between education and earnings, it's just a first step. For one thing, it captures only a moment in time. It doesn't show what a state's job market will look like when today's 18-year-olds are in their 40s. And it doesn't answer the more detailed question that many states are now struggling with: What's the precise mix of academic and nonacademic skills that best prepares young people to take advantage of labor-market opportunities?

Academic Gaps

Clearly, employers want better academic skills than many high school graduates now possess.

A survey of more than 430 human-resource officials, conducted in spring 2006 by the New York City-based Conference Board, found that 72 percent rated recent hires as deficient in basic English writing skills, such as grammar and spelling, and 81 percent rated them as deficient in written communications more broadly, such as memos, letters, and complex technical reports.

In a 2005 survey conducted for the National Association of Manufacturers, 84 percent of respondents said schools were not doing a good job preparing students for the workplace, with more than half citing specific deficiencies in mathematics and science and 38 percent citing deficiencies in reading and comprehension

Daniel Furman, the director of education policy for the nonprofit Fund for Colorado's Future, which provided staff support for a governor-appointed council to align high school standards with the demands of college and work, remembers being surprised by a representative of the Denver pipe fitters' union.

"He had just looked at 100 applications," he says, "and he mentioned they just had weak math and science skills. For a pipe fitter, perhaps you don't assume that you need individuals with strong math and science skills, but in fact you really do."

Through the American Diploma Project Network, coordinated by Achieve, 29 states have committed to aligning their high school standards with what it takes to succeed in college and the workplace. Achieve, which was formed by business leaders and state governors, has been working with 24 of those states to help them adopt high school standards that meet that goal.

Based on that work, the group has found that state standards tend to lack attention to several key areas that college faculty members and business leaders have identified as critical for success:

- While high school English standards and courses tend to emphasize literature, most of the reading material students will encounter in college or on the job is informational, such as textbooks, manuals, articles, briefs, and essays.

- While state academic-content standards tend to stress narrative writing, most of the writing young people will do in college and at work is to inform or to persuade, often requiring them to conduct research and use evidence to support a position.

- The ability to work in teams and to orally present one's work is cited by professors and employers as critical for success. Yet state standards don't always cover those skills sufficiently, according to Achieve.

On the math side of the ledger, Achieve found that state standards sometimes fall short on data analysis and statistics, and often give only superficial treatment to important geometric concepts, such as proofs. Moreover, while reasoning and solving mathematical problems are often cited as the most important skills for both college freshmen and employees, state standards don't always cover those topics explicitly.

Studies have found that students who take advanced math courses such as Algebra 2 in high school or who score higher on math tests are more likely to succeed in college and secure better-paying jobs. But some researchers and labor experts say that in many high-salary, in-demand jobs, the level of math actually needed rarely rises above the 9th or 10th grade level. Fluency in advanced math topics is less crucial, they contend, than skills in solving problems and applying math to different tasks.

College professors appear to agree. Based on a national survey of more than 6,500 middle school, high school, and postsecondary teachers, the Iowa City, Iowa-based test-maker ACT Inc. found that postsecondary instructors rated being able to understand and rigorously apply fundamental math skills and processes as more important than exposure to more advanced topics.

"The debate in states is what is the evidence that kids really need to know this stuff in the real world?" says Cohen of Achieve.

That question has led states such as Louisiana to search for examples of the specific math or English skills needed in various occupations, in part to demonstrate the relevance of state content standards to the business community.

Louisiana officials point out, for example, that to calculate drug dosages, nurses with an associate's degree need to know how to calculate and apply ratios, proportions, rates, and percentages. Nurses with a bachelor's degree must be able to select and use formal, informal, literary, or technical language appropriate for their audience so they can write formal reports to health-care managers.

"I just think there's such a lack, in textbook or curriculum guides, of 'real world' applications" of such skills, says Stanley G. Jones, Indiana's commissioner of higher education.

Soft Skills

Employers complain even more, though, about a lack of "soft" or "applied" skills among America's high school graduates than about inadequate academic skills.

In the Conference Board survey, for example, 70 percent of human-resource officials cited deficiencies among graduates in applied skills, such as professionalism and work ethic, defined as "demonstrating personal accountability and effective work habits, such as punctuality, working productively with others, time and workload management."

Similarly, in the NAM survey, 55 percent of employers rated the public education system as deficient in equipping students with basic employability skills, such as attendance, punctuality, and a strong work ethic.

Those sentiments were echoed in focus groups and round-tables that were conducted in Arkansas and Colorado with local employers.

In his state, says Furman of the Fund for Colorado's Future, employers complained that high school graduates "would not come into an interview dressed appropriately. They would not come prepared to talk about the job they were interviewing for."

"If they were lucky enough to land a job," he says, "they didn't realize they had to show up to work on time Monday through Friday."

In Arkansas, according to a January 2007 study by the Arkansas Department of Education, 76 percent of employers said recent high school graduates who applied for jobs in their companies lacked the necessary writing skills and the ability to do basic math. And more than 60 percent weren't satisfied with graduates' ability to read and understand instructions and other materials.

But the lack of soft skills—defined as everyday social skills, such as work ethic, verbal and nonverbal communications, attendance, interview abilities, and attitude—dominated the complaints of business leaders in Arkansas.

As one Arkansas employer said in a focus group, "We want somebody who shows up on time, somebody who works hard, and someone who's trainable."

James E. Rosenbaum, a sociologist at Northwestern University who's interviewed employers about their workforce needs, says, "Employers we interviewed said they were able to redesign jobs around academic-skill deficiencies, but not soft-skills deficiencies."

Nearly all jobs, he says, "require basic work habits, such as regular attendance, motivation, and discipline, and our schools are not taking steps to improve students in these areas. Indeed, the opposite may be occurring. If teachers are compelled to focus more on academic skills and test scores, they may devote less attention to soft skills and efforts to improve them."

At least one analysis, by the Princeton, N.J.-based Mathematica Policy Research Inc., suggests that improvements in nonacademic competencies—such as work habits and a belief that success results from hard work rather than luck—may be just as important for improving later earnings and postsecondary success for some students as gains in academic skills.

Using data from the National Educational Longitudinal Survey, or NELS, a federal database that followed a cohort of students from the time they were 8th graders in 1988 until 2000, the study found that for most students, improving one of the nonacademic competencies would have had a larger effect than better math scores on their chances of enrolling in and completing a postsecondary program, with 43 percent benefiting most from an improvement in work habits.

When it came to earning a bachelor's degree, however, improving math scores still had the largest effect for the most students.

In general, the Mathematica study found, students reaped the most benefit from improving in areas where they were weak. "Considering individual strengths and weaknesses when deciding which competencies to improve might be a more effective strategy than simply encouraging all students to improve the same competencies," write researchers John Deke and Joshua Haimson.

21st-Century Skills

Beyond specific content knowledge and soft skills, researchers increasingly point to a range of applied skills that span academic areas as important for success.

According to Anthony P. Carnevale, an economist and research professor at Georgetown University, individuals who score higher on measures of complex problem-solving, critical thinking, creativity, and fluency with ideas have higher mean earnings in the labor market, across all levels of education.

Individuals who score higher on measures of complex problem-solving, critical thinking, creativity, and fluency with ideas have higher mean earnings in the labor market.

David T. Conley, a professor of education at the University of Oregon, says that in addition to specific content knowledge, "a range of cognitive and meta-cognitive capabilities, often described as 'habits of mind,' have been consistently and emphatically identified by those who teach entry-level college courses as being as important or more important than any specific content knowledge taught in high school."

Examples include analysis, interpretation, precision and accuracy, problem-solving, and reasoning, he writes in "Toward a More Comprehensive Conception of College Readiness," a paper prepared for the Seattle-based Bill & Melinda Gates Foundation. Similarly important, he continues, are the attitudes and behavioral attributes that students who succeed in college demonstrate, including study skills, time management, awareness of their own performance, persistence, and the ability to use study groups.

And the Harvard University psychologist Howard Gardner, writing in his new book, *Five Minds for the Future*, defines the cognitive abilities that he argues will command a premium in the years ahead.

He describes them as the disciplinary mind (mastering ways of thinking in one or more content disciplines or a professional craft); the synthesizing mind (able to integrate ideas across disciplines and communicate that to others); the creating mind (able to uncover and clarify new problems, questions, and phenomena); the respectful mind (being aware of and appreciating differences among human beings); and the ethical mind (knowing and acting on one's responsibilities as a worker and a citizen).

Unfortunately, Gardner writes, "No one knows precisely how to fashion an education that will yield individuals who are disciplined, synthesizing, creative, respectful, and ethical."

Such skills, moreover, are hard to assess or to insert in content-oriented state high school standards.

"It's easier to get some coalescing around standards with respect to content," says Jones, the Indiana higher education commissioner. "Some of these other concepts—like working in teams, or leadership skills, or communication skills—are harder to quantify and clearly harder to assess. And so I think people recognize their importance, but they're still grappling with how you would actually do it."

More than half the employers surveyed for the Conference Board, for example, said critical thinking and problem-solving were "very important" for successful performance on the job, yet nearly three-quarters rated recent high school graduates as deficient in such skills.

Career and Technical Education

The focus on college and workforce readiness, combined with concerns about maintaining the United States' economic competitiveness, has led at least some states to place a renewed emphasis on career and technical education.

Research suggests that participation in CTE courses can reduce high school dropout rates and increase short- and medium-term earnings for students. But the research is mixed about whether participation in various types of career and technical education reduces college-going rates—or simply has no effect.

Based on analyses using students' transcript data from the National Longitudinal Survey of Youth 1997, researchers Stefanie DeLuca and Stephen Plank, sociologists at Johns Hopkins University, found that while participation in career-related programs did not generally impede college attendance, students who took proportionately more career and technical courses than academic ones were less likely to attend college, even after adjusting for other characteristics.

Moreover, while students from low-income families were the least likely to participate in career-related programs and activities, they were the most likely to take higher ratios of CTE to academic courses.

Using the same database, the Johns Hopkins researchers found that a middle-range mix of career and academic courses may decrease the risk of dropping out for students who are not over the normal age for their grades—but only up to a point, or "something in the range of one CTE course for every two core academic courses," the authors write.

They suggest trying to keep an "optimal balance" between career and academic classes, and giving students a chance to take career classes earlier, as a way to increase graduation rates.

Given that about 45 percent of high school students earned three or more occupational-course credits throughout the 1990s, the improvement of career and technical education has to be part of the "readiness" agenda, argues Richard Kazis, the director of policy for the Boston-based Jobs for the Future. But CTE programs of the future need to have greater academic rigor, be more responsive to economic trends and local labor markets, and have stronger connections to postsecondary education, he says.

Maryland, for example, has redesigned its career and technical education system around 10 career clusters, representing high-growth areas of the state's economy. More than 350 employers from across the state validated the clusters, all of which must have a postsecondary component so that students can earn at least some higher education credits while in high school.

In the 2006 graduating class, 51 percent of students who had completed a CTE program (defined as four credits in one career concentration) also had completed all the course requirements for entry into the state's four-year public colleges.

"When we first started to measure that, in 1998, it was only 14 percent," says Kathy Oliver, Maryland's assistant state superintendent for career technology and adult learning. "The goal is 100 percent, and we're moving toward that."

This past year, the National Governors Association contracted with the Monitor Group, a consulting group based in Cambridge, Mass., to produce analyses for each state of emerging, high-growth clusters.

"Cluster strategies for states are efforts to take advantage of naturally existing groupings of companies, usually within a particular industry but often including suppliers," explains Steve Crawford, who directs the NGA's division of social, economic, and workforce programs. "That sort of expertise creates a synergy in a region and gives a competitive advantage to the companies and firms."

While there is a well-established literature on the competitive advantage of clusters, he adds, "the key ingredient in any industry is knowledge or human talent, so part of a good cluster strategy is to make sure that universities, the high schools with their career academies, the community colleges, are producing folks with the skills you'd want."

PART TWO

ADVICE

"Each and every time, a new generation has risen up and done what's needed to be done. Today we are called once more—and it is time for our generation to answer that call."

BARACK OBAMA

Springfield, Ill., February 10, 2007

CHAPTER 9

Advice for the President

FROM

LINDA DARLING-HAMMOND . DAN DOMENECH
ARNE DUNCAN . MIKE FEINBERG
MARK GINSBERG . KRIS GUITIERREZ
BEVERLY HALL . ERIC HANUSHEK
RICK HESS . PHILLIP HOWARD
JACK JENNINGS . WENDY KOPP
MIRIAM KURTZIG FREEDMAN . PAUL E. LINGENFELTER
KATHLEEN MCCARTNEY . MARGARET MILLER
JOE NATHAN . MONTY NEILL
ANDREW ROTHERHAM . ALEXANDER RUSSO
TJ SINGLETARY AND KAYLIN NAZARIO
GERALD TIROZZI . MARC TUCKER

. . .

Please note that the selections in this chapter were not originally meant to appear in print. They are audio transcripts from "Education Advice for President-Elect Obama," a multimedia project that collects and distributes advice from teachers, administrators, policymakers and students and provides a platform to voice opinions, concerns and ideas about the state of U.S. education (EdAdvice ForObama.org).

The project is produced by Learning Matters, a Peabody Award-winning production company covering education issues. For more than ten years, Learning Matters has been producing outstanding reportage about American education (learningmatters.tv).

The project is supported by the Eli and Edythe Broad, Bill & Melinda Gates, Wallace, William & Flora Hewlett and Annenberg Foundations.

LINDA DARLING-HAMMOND
Charles Ducommun professor of education at Stanford University

Well, I think our next president really has to look at how we're going to bring our school system into the 21st century. We've been operating sort of on a factory model system for the last 100 years. We've also been operating the most unequal educational system in the industrialized world, with dramatically different resources available to different students. And so we're finding ourselves falling further and further behind, educationally, than other nations in the world because we're not making the kinds of investments that are necessary to ensure that all of our kids are prepared for the knowledge to work jobs that are emerging in this period of time, and also without focusing on the kinds of skills that are needed today. At this point in the knowledge economy, what kids need to be able to do is to frame and solve their own problems, find and manage information, organize themselves in teams, and—with collaboration—to tackle novel issues. It's not a matter today as it was some years ago of people going into factory model jobs and being told what to do and needing only basic rote skills to do that work. Those jobs are less than 10% of our economy now. There are very few places for people who have only a basic level of skills. So our president has to tackle this system and bring it into the 21st century. We need to focus our curriculum on standards that evaluate how people can think and problem-solve and invent and create and use knowledge in new ways and continue to learn independently. That means that we have to change the assessments that we use. Most countries in the world that are high-achieving have assessments that ask students to think and problem-solve and investigate and conduct research. We're still having our kids bubble in multiple choice test items, which focus on recall and recognition rather than these higher order thinking skills. We'll need a president who understands that we have to level the playing field in the United States. We have to give kids an equal opportunity for education. The old commitment to inequality won't get us where we need to go. That means strong investment in early childhood education because the achievement gap is very large when students enter school, particularly for low-income students who have not had the opportunity for preschool. That means we'll need to reduce the inequalities in K–12 funding. And it also means we'll have to provide much greater access to higher education. We have always been first in the world in higher education access until the last decade. And we have been slipping. Now we're 15th in the world in access because we are not providing the scholarships, forgivable loans, and other incentives that give people access to education. If they've earned their way to college, many people in America today cannot go. Meanwhile, in other countries they're building their higher education systems, and when they don't have enough slots they're sending their students to the United States on full scholarships to get educated here because they understand that that actually drives the economy back home. For every person who completes additional education, there's a net increase to the strength of the economy that is measurable and will be increasing in the years to come.

DAN DOMENECH
Executive director, American Association of School Administrators

We clearly have some suggestions and recommendations to make regarding the reauthorization of No Child Left Behind. I think the general thrust of our suggestion is to focus on poverty. Clearly the factor that most affects achievement or lack of achievement in our schools is poverty. And for years the federal government, under the Elementary and Secondary Education Act, has been spending considerable sums of money—although when you look at the total picture, it's only 8% of the typical school district's budget, but nevertheless it's a significant amount of money—that is being spent to support education at the local level. However, the problem is that what started out back in 1965 as just a couple of programs has now grown to as many as 93 different grants programs that are scattered all over the place with little focus and little coordination. And we feel that if the new president were to take those programs and consolidate them and focus them on poverty—the issue of poverty—which is the biggest factor in the schools, that we would see greater efficiency and greater effectiveness in terms of achievement level, and closing that achievement gap which continues to be such a big issue.

ARNE DUNCAN
CEO of the Chicago Public Schools

My advice for the next president, who I fervently hope will be Barack Obama, will be to continue to go on the path that he's been moving. On the early childhood education side, Senator Obama has been proposing a couple of things: one is to dramatically increase the number of seats available to dramatically increase access. Investing in children early has to happen if you want them to have a chance at having successful futures. That's hugely important. But at the same time he coupled that with upgrading quality. This can't just be babysitting, and so he set some pretty high goals . . . high standards for teaching quality. On the higher education side, there are two things that he's working on that I think are fascinating. One is trying to really make that first $4,000 basically free for any student wanting to go to college as long as they're willing to do 100 hours of community service. I think the coupling of those opportunities as well as a sort of giving back—that community service aspect, that reciprocity—is hugely powerful. And then secondly, I think at the back end, he's talked a lot about giving scholarships or loans to folks that go into public service, whether it's teaching or other things. And commit to that for four or five years after college. This has to be a comprehensive plan; you can't do one without the other. So these are all pieces of a larger puzzle.

MIKE FEINBERG
Co-Founder of the KIPP (Knowledge Is Power Program)
Foundation and the superintendent of KIPP Houston

I'd love to see the next president work on highly qualified teachers. I think having highly qualified teachers is a very important and noble goal. Unfortunately, it's just wound up getting interpreted as highly certified teachers. I'd like us to have a common language on what we think excellent teaching and learning looks like. And we make it very easy for people who can be great teachers and help kids become great learners to get into the classroom—quickly—to help all of our children. I'd also like us to become a United States (emphasize the United) in terms of standards. Instead of having 50 different states with 50 different standards, I'd love to see the next president unify the country to have a common vision of what excellent teaching, excellent learning looks like. To prepare our children for success in the future, having one set of standards and having one way to measure how kids in schools and districts and states are progressing against those standards. It's going to require a multi-state effort. I think if we sit back and wait, though, whether we decide the federal government should work on that, or the state government should work on that, or local school districts should work on that, people are going to be pointing the finger at each other. This is where I think we require leadership more than ever. At some level somebody's got to say, "Stop the madness. Enough is enough!" Let's get a bunch of people together over a period of time to knock out standards that this country can live with, the states can live with, the cities can live with, the districts can live with, and most importantly the parents, who when they look at the report cards of their kid, they can know that what's being measured is what their kids need to learn to set them up for success in the future.

MARK GINSBERG
*Executive director, National Association for
the Education of Young Children*

My advice for the next president is to be deliberate, strategic, and very strong in providing for funding so that every American child receives a quality education—a quality education that begins at birth and continues as the child grows and develops into an adult. Sometimes when we speak of pre-K, we talk about four-year-olds or three-year-olds, but we know that learning begins much earlier than that. And in fact, the systems providing for early education in this country are systems that are fractured and not accessible widely enough to every child in the country. The foundations for learning should begin very, very early in life, and when we see so many of our children not succeeding over the course of their formal learning experience in the Pre-K–12 system, we have to go back and kind of ask the question, "Why?" Why is it that so many of our children aren't ready for school? Why is it that many of our schools aren't ready for all of our children? I think our failure to provide an adequate, high-quality education across the childhood and adolescent years begins with our failure to provide an accessible, affordable, high-quality education very early in life that sows the seeds of success.

KRIS GUITIERREZ

Professor of social research methodology at the Graduate School of Education and Information Studies at UCLA

As an educator, I would really love the next president to change the discourse in education. One that would bring us to "What is the fundamental role of education in the democracy?" And that would mean, of course, tying education to health care, to work, and to the everyday lives of people in ways that remind us again what the fundamental purpose of schooling is in a democracy. So, I would want to really help them make those connections instead of telegraphing these individual policies about fixing this and changing that. Some larger coherent vision about the moral and political and social role of education in a democracy. I think that's just fundamental. And it's a discourse that's been lost in the discourses of deficit and failure of students and failures of teachers. I come from a very small mining town in Arizona from modest means. And I think that I would turn to the kinds of questions my parents would have asked because I think that really reminds me—not just as an educator—what good, hard-working people are really looking for in an educational system. And even though we were from poor mining communities, education was really a right and a privilege in our community and we all had access to a rich curriculum in humanities and music and the arts . . . and the opportunity to develop the habits of mind that fostered a love of learning. So I know it's possible, not just in high-income areas, but in working-class areas. Thinking about my parents, my working-class parents, I would want to know so much more about what education means from my president. And will the kind of vision of education get me to the next level? Will it give me an opportunity to be in high-status courses? Will it prepare me to go to any university and college in the country? You know, my tiny small town had one of the highest-going college-bound rates in all the state of Arizona. And I think it's because the whole community really understood the value of education, in terms of—not just up-ward mobility—but in terms of the common good.

BEVERLY HALL
Superintendent of Atlanta Public Schools

I have a few pieces of advice to the next president of the United States. The first has to do with the establishment of national educa-tion standards. As the world becomes increasingly small and Amer-ica's high school and college graduates are competing for jobs with students from around the world, the president of the United States must take a leadership role in setting national educational standards. He should clearly articulate what the nation expects our children to know and to be able to do, he should develop standards that are competitive with those anywhere in the world, and he should insist that the state testing systems are realigned with those standards.

ERIC HANUSHEK
*Paul and Jean Hanna senior fellow at the
Hoover Institution of Stanford University*

I think the most important thing for the next president to understand is that the quality of our K–12 education system has an enormous impact on the future economic well-being of people in the United

States. So this means that we can't just sit back and do things as we've been doing. The president can, in fact, take a leadership position to improve and strengthen the accountability systems that are in the various states. There's been a lot of discussion about NCLB over the last year or two. Much of this discussion has focused on some of the flaws or problems with the current system. Those flaws are real, but the truth of the matter is that the system—even with its flaws—has improved schooling in our states. Moreover, a number of these flaws can be fixed. It's not a matter of, because there's flaws we should get rid of the system. It's instead, because there's flaws, we should improve it to provide the guidance that is needed and provide the overall national commitment to high student performance.

RICK HESS
Director of education policy studies at the
American Enterprise Institute in Washington, D.C.

I think there are probably four things for the next president to focus on. One is trying to get the federal role in accountability straightened out. Rather than creating this immense maze of rules and regulations governing accountability and state assessments, it makes more sense to have clear benchmarks and assessments and then create a lot more flexibility for states to react to that data. So the second piece of it is to get out of the business of micromanaging state and district improvement strategies. The third is to think of a federal role in providing support and political cover for states and districts that are trying to move forward in innovative ways to solve problems more effectively. And the fourth piece is to help identify where anachronistic federal or state policies are getting in the way of dynamic problem solving.

PHILLIP HOWARD
Founder and president of Common Good,
a nonprofit, nonpartisan legal reform coalition

If I were advising the president about what to do with American education, I would tell him to please get rid of the bureaucracy and the law and let people take back control of the schools. The first thing he could do is get rid of No Child Left Behind and replace it with just a national testing standard, but none of the bells and whistles. If this happens, and you don't achieve annual yearly progress, then you lose this funding, and you have the right to go to that school. Let the accountability mechanisms be local. I think trying to tell people, trying to manage from the top what's an effective educational system has proven to be a nightmare. No one's ever shown it to work. I think the president has to have a bully pulpit to try to create a New Deal for teachers because everyone knows that the bureaucratic constraints don't just come from the boards of education, they also come through 200-page teachers union contracts. So there's a deal to be made here, and someone has to take the leadership to create the new deal that re-professionalizes teachers but also allows the administrators, principals, and others to manage the schools, and that includes judging who's effective and who isn't.

JACK JENNINGS
President and CEO of the nonpartisan Center on Education Policy

My advice for the new president is to take action in three areas: first and most importantly, he should restore the economy, because schools rely on local property taxes for their operation and they also rely on state income and state sales taxes for their basic operation. And when the economy is not doing well, the basic support for the schools is shaky. So that's the first order of priority—make sense out of this economy. The second order of priority is to fix the No Child Left Behind Act. That act holds schools accountable in a way that is not generally accepted by teachers, and the accountability mechanism must be changed to identify whether schools are doing well and whether students are increasing in academic achievement. That act also needs to be fixed because once schools are identified for help, they're not being provided the assistance they need to improve. And teachers are not provided with the assistance they need to become better teachers. So there's a need to round out the act, not only to the accountability mechanism—but the mechanism that actually provides assistance to schools and teachers. The third thing a president should do is to think about before school and after elementary/secondary school. And before school, there's a need to improve the quality of preschool education. Right now there's multiple opportunities for early childhood education, but the quality is very, very uneven, so many kids are coming to school without adequately being prepared for elementary school. And then at the other end of the spectrum, once kids leave high school, they're finding that they can't always afford college. So there should be serious attention to helping parents and students to be able to afford college, so that everyone who wants to go to college would be able to go. So that's my advice to the president, three tall orders, but if the president's able to address these three, I think we're all better off as a country.

WENDY KOPP
Founder and president of Teach for America

I think the next president has a true opportunity to build a set of reforms on the basis of what we now know is working in communities. And I hope they decide to prioritize that, and to pick a secretary of education who deeply understands the policies and is brilliant about the politics. So I think one of the questions we need to consider is, "How do we generate still greater local commitment, local leadership, local initiatives to work on behalf of insuring that all kids do have the chance to obtain an excellent education? I think we need to call up on people from all backgrounds, in all honesty. And I think the role of alternative programs for recruiting teachers and school principals as well as district leaders is one means of doing that. I think our school systems need to recruit aggressively from all sectors—certainly from our education schools, but as far beyond that as they need to go to find truly talented, committed folks to work as teachers, as school leaders, and district administrators.

MIRIAM KURTZIG FREEDMAN
*Attorney, expert, and author, who has spoken on
education law and strategy in 45 states*

Our special ed law started in the 1950s because back then, many students with disabilities, about a million of them, were excluded from school. The issue then was access to programming for all children. The law provided new funding, new direction, and due process rights for parents. It was a new day. Many of us—educators, administrators, taxpayers, parents—have come to the unsettling realization that the system struggles and is unsustainable. Burdensome requirements take teachers and students away from the mission: teaching and learning. We spend some 80 billion dollars on special ed, yet the budgetary system has not kept with the times because special ed costs protected by federal law often impact other school programs and reforms. I would tell the president that, as sad as it is, even though we met the access challenges of the '70s, this law has not changed. And I think some courage to step up to the plate is what's needed.

PAUL E. LINGENFELTER
*President of the National Association of
State Higher Education Executives*

The United States needs to generate another 16 million college graduates in the next 16 years, and the president is going to have to lead us by making that a national priority. The federal government can't do the whole work, but the federal government can do some things to simplify student aid to provide more assistance to adult students so they can focus on a program and succeed. We need to improve education which came in through K–12, but if you dig into the numbers you'll discover that we can't generate more than 30% of those 16 million degrees by increasing high school graduation rates, college participation, and college graduation rates by ten percentage points.

KATHLEEN MCCARTNEY
Dean of the Harvard Graduate School of Education

The main piece of advice I would have for the next president is this: too often educational policy is dictated by opinion and ideology rather than by research. School districts need to be able to make data-driven decisions. Unfortunately, there are limited federal funds available for education, and for that reason we must be sure that every dollar is spent effectively. I realize that this might be politically difficult for the next president because the benefits of the research would likely be reaped upon his successor. But if we are truly going to solve some of the enormous education challenges facing the country, we must have solid education research to guide our decisions. Second piece of advice I would give to the president is to really use the bully pulpit to put education front and center, and to build public will to do something. I think it's especially important to have a president who can talk to parents and not just teachers, about what parents could do to support their kids. The president should be telling parents to turn off the television, to help their children find a quiet place to study, and parents should be checking their children's homework. We need to help them understand that doing well in school sets the stage for life success.

MARGARET MILLER
*Professor in the Center for the Study of Higher
Education at the University of Virginia*

My advice to the next president of the United States is that he recognize that higher education is the key to national welfare and our position in the world. We used to be a financial leader in the world. We're now slipping on that front. We used to be an educational leader in the world, and that too is an area in which we're slipping. We used to be a research leader, and we now are no longer that either. I think there are now a number of things that we need to do—or that the president needs to do—and one is to use the power of the purse to fund basic research and access to higher education for students. I think he needs to use the bully pulpit to reach out to lower-income and disadvantaged potential students and support their success. I think he also could speak to the importance of community colleges and historically Black colleges and universities, Hispanic-serving institutions, and tribal colleges in their contribution to the education of minority students. And I think that the most important thing he needs to do is keep his eye on the achievement gap between majority and minority students in this country. Overall, our baccalaureate attainment levels in 2005 were 86% of Norway's, which is the best-performing OECD nation. But our attainment rates are only 40% and 60% of the best practice rate of African-American men and women, and only 30% and 40% for Hispanic men and women. So attainment rates among white men are almost as high as Norwegians; for white women they are as high. So those differences are what is the root of our problem in this country. The next president needs to be sure that whatever he does, he gives support to students of color and disadvantaged populations of students and supports their success.

JOE NATHAN
Director of the Center for School Change
at the University of Minnesota

Here are the five priorities. First, I would establish a handful of clear, specific, measurable goals for the next six to ten years. Secondly, I would encourage the replication of outstanding district and charter schools throughout the United States. Third, I would give highly successful inner-city, suburban, and rural public schools the opportunity to train the next generation of school teachers and administrators, and I would set up some competition. I would create new and hopefully more-effective teacher preparation and administrator preparation programs based in outstanding schools. And we can talk about the definition of outstanding schools. Fourth, I would dramatically expand high-quality early childhood educational programs, and finally I would encourage states, through incentives and other forms of assistance, to rethink whether we really need to have students in elementary and secondary school, kindergarten through 12, and then wait until kids are 18 or 19 before they go to colleges and universities. I think we could save literally millions of dollars, and I think many, many are ready for much more challenging opportunities at 16 or 17. So those are my five priorities.

MONTY NEILL
*Deputy director of Fair Test, the national
center for fair and open testing*

Our recommendations to the president cover three interrelated and broad areas. The first is opportunity to learn and resources for schools. The second is improvement factors and how to help schools actually improve. And the third is the need for far-improved assessment. The current situation, as we know, is that many school are inadequately resourced, and those are typically schools serving children who come from low-income communities, and that both the lack of resources and support in communities and in schools make it very difficult for those children to effectively and successfully learn academics in schools. We need significantly stepped-up federal support—financial support— for education for low-income children, quite possibly some form of in effect guaranteeing that the authorized funds for IDEA or No Child Left Behind are, in fact, appropriated and spent. In other words, both of those should be what we call fully funded. And our advice to the president would be to pay attention to all of these factors and lead the way in creating a new Elementary and Secondary Education Act to replace No Child Left Behind.

ANDREW ROTHERHAM
*Co-founder and co-director of Education Sector, an
independent national education policy think tank*

My advice for the next president is to be very flexible about means, but at the same time be absolutely firm about ends. The next president is going to have to be very creative about doing more with less.

Again the resource picture is very tight, and we're not going to be able to spend our way out of this problem, as we've often, traditionally, have or tried to in education policy. There are concerns about everything from recruiting and preparation and training of teachers to how they're compensated. And we've got to do something about pre-K, that sort of uneven patchwork of support for kids before they come into kindergarten, and especially for low-income kids and students of color. Then the final thing is both research and development and innovation. And traditionally research and development in education has been very weak—both in under-investment and a lack of capacity—and really, more broadly, just a lack of incentives around it. There are a lot of opportunities for the next administration to take on those areas of policy. This is not a time to sort of throw up our hands and say, "We can't do this" because the economic picture is kind of bleak. It's actually a great time to sort of double down around some of these hard choices and to really take those on.

ALEXANDER RUSSO

Freelance education writer and creator and editor of the popular education blog, This Week in Education. He also blogs at District 299: The Chicago Schools Blog.

My advice for the next president is that he doesn't wimp out on No Child Left Behind. There are a lot of people who want to do more than fix it . . . they want to gut it. And I hope that next president doesn't do that. I hope that the next president finds a way to make states and districts admit how much financial support they're getting from No Child Left Behind and federal programs in general. They often act like they don't get very much money from the feds, when in fact they get a lot of money. And I wish there was a way to make them admit that, so that they couldn't bash the law and take the money at the same time. My other advice to the next president is not to reinvent Head Start under the guise of universal preschool. We've got a giant Head Start program. It would be a shame to bypass revising and improving that program while we're creating universal preschool. And it would be an extra shame if we had two massive federal programs that didn't coordinate with each other or overlap each other. Last, but not least, I'd say the next president should ignore 90% of what the pointy-headed wonks in DC tell you to do. Most of them are just promoting their own ideas or their own ideology. Talk to teachers and talk to principals, and you'll get the best advice.

TJ SINGLETARY AND KAYLIN NAZARIO
Students at Vanguard High School in New York City

TJ SINGLETARY: I'm TJ. I go to Vanguard High School. I'm 15, and I'm a sophomore.

KAYLIN NAZARIO: I'm Kaylin. I go to Vanguard High School also. I'm in 11th grade, and I live in Manhattan.

TJS: I feel that in school we have good education, but there's nothing to do after school, and I think that's a lot because of the budget cuts that are happening. If kids were able to have extra-curriculum activities, some of the things that were going on outside of school wouldn't be happening as often.

KN: I think teachers and the school in general deserves more funding so that we can have more supplies. Calculators we don't have, in math, right, we like have to share. And you know, textbooks, like that kinds of thing. You could probably send some more money our way. That could probably help out.

TJS: I think that they should work a lot on the younger people because that's the next generation. Those are the people who are going to vote the next years, and they should have an education, and they should be aware of what's going on in the world.

GERALD TIROZZI
*Executive director of the National Association
of Secondary School Principals*

Well, for the next president, I fully understand and appreciate all the economic, social, environmental, war-related issues he's going to face. But I would sincerely hope that he could figure out a way to elevate education to a much higher priority than it has received over the past year, especially during the presidential campaign. You know, there are many issues in our schools that need to be resolved, and I don't think we can wait two to three years to regain our priority status. We talk about the economy and getting the economy better. Education—public education in particular—is one of the real drivers of the economy. And when you consider the fact that we have a significant dropout problem in this country—we have a significant number of kids who don't finish school—we have to figure these issues out, and it's really going to take resources. No Child Left Behind, for all of its problems, at least was leading us in a direction that I think was okay, but it was never fully funded. You know we have the special ed. mandates that were never fully funded. So I think when you layer on more mandates on the schools, and at the same time you're not providing the requisite resources, it's like you have a vision which becomes a hallucination. You need resources. The president has a bully pulpit. If he tells Congress this is important, I think they listen to him. I'm also pleased both candidates have said that they support the full funding of IDEA (Individuals with Disabilities Education Act). Now if both are saying that and one of them will become president, you would like to think they will fulfill that promise. I don't think it can happen overnight, but in a reasonable period of time. You know, that was a promise made in '76—that they would fund 40% of the excess cost of special education—and right now we're 22 or 23 years later, and they're only funding 17%. So you know that burden's been picked up by the schools. I think that's very unfair, and I would really hope the president, whoever it is, would take that one on.

MARC TUCKER

President, National Center on Education and the Economy (NCEE)

The United States operates one of the highest-cost, lowest-performing elementary and secondary education systems in the industrialized world. Our research and that of others shows that this is because of the dysfunctional design of the American education system. What we need is a system that is able to attract its teachers from the top third of all our college graduates, as the best-performing nations do. That requires much higher compensation and, even more important, redefining the job of the teachers along professional, not blue collar, lines. That means putting the teachers in charge of our schools, just as doctors, attorneys, architects, and others are in charge of their own practices. That will require us to redesign our systems of management, accountability, and organization along modern professional lines, too. If we succeed, the new system will not look much like the current one, which was designed a century ago to meet very different challenges than the ones we face now. That is true not least because we can get there only by redeploying a substantial portion of the money we are now spending on our schools, rather than spending even more than we do now. President-elect Obama has an opportunity to lead this process of redesign. There is not a moment to lose. The United States used to have the best-educated workforce in the world. Now we are number 10 and sinking. We don't need a national ministry of education. But we do need someone who can articulate what is at stake and a clear vision of what might be. No one is better qualified to do this than the president-elect.

CHAPTER 10

National Academy of Education Recommendations

THE NATIONAL ACADEMY OF EDUCATION (NAEd) advances the highest quality education research and its use in policy formation and practice. Founded in 1965, the Academy consists of U.S. members and foreign associates who are elected on the basis of outstanding scholarship or contributions to education. Since its establishment, the Academy has undertaken numerous commissions and study panels which typically include both NAEd members and other scholars with expertise in a particular area of inquiry.

In 2008, The National Academy of Education undertook an initiative to connect policymakers in a new administration and Congress with the best available evidence on selected education policy issues. The project was designed to help policymakers better understand key education issues and to strengthen their ability to formulate effective policies by providing them with independent, research-based information.

The findings from the resulting white papers were presented on November 18, 2008. Each of the white papers addresses one of six key areas in education policy:

- Reading and literacy
- Science and mathematics education
- Time for learning
- Teacher quality
- Standards, assessments, and accountability
- Equity and excellence in American education

Each paper reviews the available research evidence and presents possible policy options or recommendations. They were subjected to a rigorous peer review process before being released, both to ensure the highest quality and to vet the evidentiary basis for the conclusions and recommendations. The full text can read at www. naeducation.org. The recommendations are excerpted below.

Literacy for Learning

Recommendation: State and federal governments should increase investment in early education programs and make oral language development a primary focus of preschool.

Recommendation: The United States should make it a national priority to provide English language learners with targeted, conceptually rich language instruction starting in preschool and continuing until students are fully proficient in English.

World-Class Science and Mathematics

Recommendation: The federal government-working with consortia of states, should invest in the creation of model instructional packages to help schools develop their capacity to teach 21st-century science and mathematics skills from kindergarten through grade eight.

Recommendation: Study effective teaching practice in science and mathematics at all grade levels and use that knowledge to recommend specific improvements in teacher preparation programs.

Recommendation: The federal government should play a leading role in encouraging and providing resources for engineering design and research cycles to support the improvement of education, including in science and mathematics.

Improving Teacher Quality and Distribution

Recommendation: States, school districts, and the federal government should continue to experiment with a variety of teacher recruitment programs, while collecting data to be used to improve those that are promising and end those that are not.

Recommendation: States and the federal government should continue to fund experiments that examine the full range of possibilities designed to increase teacher retention, including salary incentives for successful teachers, improvements in working conditions and school culture, and mentoring and professional development.

Time: A Precious Resource for Learning

Recommendation: Identify, support, and test promising policies to increase the enrollment and regular attendance of disadvantaged students in summer school programs.

Recommendation: Working together, federal and state governments, business groups, and philanthropies should fund efforts to develop and test effective models of after-school programs that can be successfully implemented in a wide variety of community settings.

Recommendation: Fund and carefully evaluate the costs and benefits of pilot programs that greatly expand schooling time.

Recovering the Promise of Standards-based Education

Recommendation: The federal government should encourage the redesign of content standards—and the curricula, professional development, and assessments that must go with them—to present clear progressions for teaching and learning. Efforts to develop these instructional systems may involve partnerships among states, universities, groups of teachers, scholars, and the private sector.

Recommendation: The federal government should support a program of research and development of the next generation of assessment tools and strategies for accountability systems.

Equity and Excellence in American Education

Recommendation: The federal government should invest in strategies that are supported by research evidence to increase educational opportunity and excellence for all students across their school career.

Recommendation: The federal government should support and develop information systems that can be used by policymakers, education practitioners, and others to monitor education progress and accountability.

The National Academy of Education White Papers Project is supported through a grant provided by Rockefeller Philanthropy Advisors in conjunction with its sponsorship of Strong American Schools, a nonpartisan campaign supported by The Eli and Edythe Broad Foundation and the Bill & Melinda Gates Foundation to promote sound education policies for all Americans. Any opinions, findings, conclusions, or recommendations expressed here do not necessarily reflect the views of the project funder.

The Obama-Biden Education Plan

BARACK OBAMA AND JOE BIDEN believe that our kids and our country can't afford four more years of neglect and indifference. At this defining moment in our history, America faces few more urgent challenges than preparing our children to compete in a global economy. The decisions our leaders make about education in the coming years will shape our future for generations to come. Obama and Biden are committed to meeting this challenge with the leadership and judgment that has been sorely lacking for the last eight years. Their vision for a 21st-century education begins with demanding more reform and accountability, coupled with the resources needed to carry out that reform; asking parents to take responsibility for their children's success; and recruiting, retaining, and rewarding an army of new teachers to fill new successful schools that prepare our children for success in college and the workforce. The Obama-Biden plan will restore the promise of America's public education, and ensure that American children again lead the world in achievement, creativity, and success.

Early Childhood Education

- **Zero to Five Plan:** The Obama-Biden comprehensive "Zero to Five" plan will provide critical support to young children and their parents. Unlike other early childhood education plans, the Obama-Biden plan places key emphasis at early care and education for infants, which is essential for children to be ready to enter kindergarten. Obama and Biden will create Early Learning Challenge Grants to promote state Zero to Five efforts and help states move toward voluntary, universal preschool.

- **Expand Early Head Start and Head Start:** Obama and Biden will quadruple Early Head Start, increase Head Start funding, and improve quality for both.

- **Provide affordable, High-Quality Child Care:** Obama and Biden will also increase access to affordable and high-quality child care to ease the burden on working families.

K–12

- **Reform No Child Left Behind:** Obama and Biden will reform NCLB, which starts by funding the law. Obama and Biden believe teachers should not be forced to spend the academic year preparing students to fill in bubbles on standardized tests. They will improve the assessments used to track student progress to measure readiness for college and the workplace and improve student learning in a timely, individualized manner. Obama and Biden will also improve NCLB's accountability system so that we are supporting schools that need improvement, rather than punishing them.

- **Support High-Quality Schools and Close Low-Performing Charter Schools:** Barack Obama and Joe Biden will double funding for the Federal Charter School Program to support the creation of more successful charter schools. The Obama-Biden administration will provide this expanded charter school funding only to states that improve accountability for charter schools, allow for interventions in struggling charter schools, and have a clear process for closing down chronically underperforming charter schools. Obama and Biden will also prioritize supporting states that help the most successful charter schools to expand to serve more students.

- **Make Math and Science Education a National Priority:** Obama and Biden will recruit math and science degree graduates to the teaching profession and will support efforts to help these teachers learn from professionals in the field. They will also work to ensure that all children have access to a strong science curriculum at all grade levels.

- **Address the Dropout Crisis:** Obama and Biden will address the dropout crisis by passing legislation to provide funding to school districts to invest in intervention strategies in middle school—strategies such as personal academic plans, teaching teams, parent involvement, mentoring, intensive reading and math instruction, and extended learning time.

- **Expand High-Quality After-School Opportunities:** Obama and Biden will double funding for the main federal support for after-school programs, the 21st Century Learning Centers program, to serve one million more children.

- **Support College Outreach Programs:** Obama and Biden support outreach programs like GEAR UP, TRIO, and Upward Bound to encourage more young people from low-income families to consider and prepare for college.

- **Support College Credit Initiatives:** Barack Obama and Joe Biden will create a national "Make College A Reality" initiative that has a bold goal to increase students taking AP or college-level classes nationwide 50 percent by 2016, and will build on Obama's bipartisan proposal in the U.S. Senate to provide grants for students seeking college level credit at community colleges if their school does not provide those resources.

- **Support English Language Learners:** Obama and Biden support transitional bilingual education and will help limited-English-proficient students get ahead by holding schools accountable for making sure these students complete school.

- **Recruit Teachers:** Obama and Biden will create new Teacher Service Scholarships that will cover four years of undergraduate or two years of graduate teacher education, including high-quality alternative programs for mid-career recruits in exchange for teaching for at least four years in a high-need field or location.

- **Prepare Teachers:** Obama and Biden will require all schools of education to be accredited. Obama and Biden will also create a voluntary national performance assessment so we can be sure that every new educator is trained and ready to walk into the classroom and start teaching effectively. Obama and Biden will also create Teacher Residency Programs that will supply 30,000 exceptionally well-prepared recruits to high-need schools.

- **Retain Teachers:** To support our teachers, the Obama-Biden plan will expand mentoring programs that pair experienced teachers with new recruits. They will also provide incentives to give teachers paid common planning time so they can collaborate to share best practices.

- **Reward Teachers:** Obama and Biden will promote new and innovative ways to increase teacher pay that are developed with teachers, not imposed on them. Districts will be able to design programs that reward with a salary increase accomplished educators who serve as mentors to new teachers. Districts can reward teachers who work in underserved places like rural areas and inner cities. And if teachers consistently excel in the classroom, that work can be valued and rewarded as well.

Higher Education

- **Create the American Opportunity Tax Credit:** Obama and Biden will make college affordable for all Americans by creating a new American Opportunity Tax Credit. This universal and fully refundable credit will ensure that the first $4,000 of a college education is completely free for most Americans, and will cover two-thirds the cost of tuition at the average public college or university and make community college tuition completely free for most students. Recipients of the credit will be required to conduct 100 hours of community service.

- **Simplify the Application Process for Financial Aid:** Obama and Biden will streamline the financial aid process by eliminating the current federal financial aid application and enabling families to apply simply by checking a box on their tax form, authorizing their tax information to be used, and eliminating the need for a separate application.

Support Students with Disabilities

Obama and Biden will work to ensure the academic success of students with disabilities by increasing funding and effectively enforcing the Individuals with Disabilities Education Act, and by holding schools accountable for providing students with disabilities the services and supports they need to reach their potential. Obama and Biden will also support Early Intervention services for infants and toddlers, and will work to improve college opportunities for high school graduates with disabilities.

www.change.gov

Education Week Commentary Contributors

Chapter 1

Samuel J. Meisels is the president of the Erikson Institute in Chicago.

Lawrence J. Schweinhart has conducted research at the High/Scope Educational Research Foundation (www.highscope.org) in Ypsilanti, Mich., since 1975, and has served as its president since 2003.

Chapter 2

Thomas E. Petri, a member of the U.S. House of Representatives from Wisconsin, is a former vice chairman of the Education and Labor Committee and a senior Republican on the committee.

Richard D. Kahlenberg, a senior fellow at the Century Foundation in Washington, is the editor of *Improving on No Child Left Behind: Getting Education Reform Back on Track.*

Chapter 3

Richard Whitmire is an editorial writer for *USA Today* and the president of the Education Writers Association. Andrew J. Rotherham is a co-director of Education Sector and a member of the Virginia state board of education. He writes the blog Eduwonk.com.

Ted Mitchell is the chief executive officer of the San Francisco-based philanthropy NewSchools Venture Fund and the president of the California state board of education. Jonathan Schorr is a partner at the NewSchools Venture Fund.

Chapter 4

Coverage of mathematics, science, and technology education is supported by a grant from the Ewing Marion Kauffman Foundation, at www.kauffman.org.

Chapter 5

Cheryl Almeida is a program director and Adria Steinberg is an associate vice president at Jobs for the Future, a nonprofit research and advocacy organization in Boston.

Chapter 7

James W. Guthrie is a professor of public policy and education; the chair of the department of leadership, policy, and organizations; and the director of the Peabody Center for Education Policy at Vanderbilt University's Peabody College, in Nashville, Tenn. Patrick J. Schuermann is a research assistant professor at Peabody College.

Julie Sweetland is a senior research associate at the Center for Inspired Teaching, in Washington.

Arthur E. Levine is the president and David Haselkorn is a senior fellow of the Woodrow Wilson National Fellowship Foundation, in Princeton, N.J.

Linda Darling-Hammond is the Charles E. Ducommun professor of education at Stanford University.

Index

This page constitutes an extension of the copyright page.
Grateful acknowledgment is made for permission to print the following:

CHAPTER I

"Long-Term Payoff Seen From Early-Childhood Education," by Linda Jacobson, as first appeared in *Education Week*, June 11, 2008. Reprinted with permission from Editorial Projects in Education.
"Pre-K Study Shows Good and Bad News," by Linda Jacobson, as first appeared in *Education Week*, March 26, 2008. Reprinted with permission from Editorial Projects in Education.
"Fine-Tuning Preschool Rating Systems," by Linda Jacobson, as first appeared in *Education Week*, October 29, 2008. Reprinted with permission from Editorial Projects in Education.
"Preschool Education and Its Lasting Effects," by Linda Jacobson, as first appeared in *Education Week*, September 17, 2008. Reprinted with permission from Editorial Projects in Education.
"Teacher-Pupil Link Crucial to Pre-K Success," by Linda Jacobson, as first appeared in *Education Week*, May 21, 2008. Reprinted with permission from Editorial Projects in Education.
"Universal Pre-K: What About the Babies?" by Samuel J. Meisels, as first appeared in *Education Week*, January 25, 2006. Reprinted with permission from Editorial Projects in Education.
"Creating the Best Prekindergartens: Five Ingredients for Long-Term Effects and Returns on Investment," by Lawrence Schweinhart, as first appeared in *Education Week*, March 19, 2008. Reprinted with permission from Editorial Projects in Education.

CHAPTER 2

"NCLB Testing Said to Give 'Illusions of Progress,'" by Scott J. Cech, as first appeared in *Education Week*, September 22, 2008. Reprinted with permission from Editorial Projects in Education.
"Top Students Said to Stagnate Under NCLB," by Debra Viadero, as first appeared in *Education Week*, June 18, 2008. Reprinted with permission from Editorial Projects in Education.
Definition of "NCLB" from *The* EDUCATION WEEK *Guide to K–12 Terminology* (Jossey-Bass). Copyright © 2008 by Editorial Projects in Education. Reprinted with permission.
"Schools Found Likely to Miss NCLB Targets," by Sean Cavanagh & David Hoff, as first appeared in *Education Week*, October 1, 2008. Reprinted with permission from Editorial Projects in Education.
"City Leaders Back Stronger Accountability," by David Hoff, as first appeared in *Education Week*, July 30, 2008. Reprinted with permission from Editorial Projects in Education.
"Where's the 'Child' in the No Child Left Behind Debate?" by Thomas E. Petri, as first appeared in *Education Week*, February 4, 2008. Reprinted with permission from Editorial Projects in Education.
"What to Do With No Child Left Behind?" by Richard D. Kahlenberg, as first appeared in *Education Week*, October 15, 2008. Reprinted with permission from Editorial Projects in Education.

CHAPTER 3

"Edge Seen for Chicago Charter High Schools," by Debra Viadero, as first appeared in *Education Week*, May 14, 2008. Reprinted with permission from Editorial Projects in Education.
Definition of "Charter Schools" from *The Education Week Guide to K–12 Terminology* (Jossey-Bass). Copyright © 2008 by Editorial Projects in Education. Reprinted with permission.
"NAEP Gap Continuing for Charters," by Erik W. Robelen, as first appeared in *Education Week*, May 21, 2008. Reprinted with permission from Editorial Projects in Education.
"'Green' Charters Forge a Network," by Erik W. Robelen, as first appeared in *Education Week*, November 28, 2007. Reprinted with permission from Editorial Projects in Education.
"In New Orleans, University's Charter School Makes Gains," by Lesli A. Maxwell, as first appeared in *Education Week*, May 21, 2008. Reprinted with permission from Editorial Projects in Education.
"A Defining Moment for Charter Schools?" by Richard Whitmire & Andrew J. Rotherham, as first appeared in *Education Week*, February 13, 2008. Reprinted with permission from Editorial Projects in Education.
"Federal Education Innovation—Getting It Right," by Ted Mitchell & Jonathan Schorr, as first appeared in *Education Week*, October 29, 2008. Reprinted with permission from Editorial Projects in Education.

CHAPTER 4

"Asians Best U.S. Students in Math and Science," by Kathleen Kennedy Manzo, as first appeared in *Education Week*, December 9, 2008. Reprinted with permission from Editorial Projects in Education.
"Science Education," by Mary C. Breadon, as first appeared in *Education Week*, March 26, 2008. Reprinted with permission from Editorial Projects in Education.
"Scientists Nurture Teachers' Growth in Math and Science," by Sean Cavanagh, as first appeared in *Education Week*, November 28, 2007. Reprinted with permission from Editorial Projects in Education.
"Labs at Elementary Level Help Bring Science Alive," by Sean Cavanagh, as first appeared in

Education Week, June 4, 2008. Reprinted with permission from Editorial Projects in Education. "A School Where STEM Is King," by Andrew Trotter, as first appeared in *Education Week*, March 27, 2008. Reprinted with permission from Editorial Projects in Education.

CHAPTER 5
"Motivating Students in the Middle Years," by Kathleen Kennedy Manzo, as first appeared in *Education Week*, March 19, 2008. Reprinted with permission from Editorial Projects in Education.
"Middle School Performance," by Debra Viadero, as first appeared in *Education Week*, February 6, 2008. Reprinted with permission from Editorial Projects in Education.
"Chicago Students to Play Lead Role in Dropout Project," by Catherine Gewertz, as first appeared in *Education Week*, November 19, 2008. Reprinted with permission from Editorial Projects in Education.
"Instructional Model May Yield Gains for English-Learners," by May Ann Zehr, as first appeared in *Education Week*, December 5, 2007. Reprinted with permission from Editorial Projects in Education.
"Dropout Prevention," by Mary C. Breaden, as first appeared in *Education Week*, November 14, 2007. Reprinted with permission from Editorial Projects in Education.
"Raising Graduation Rates in an Era of High Standards," by Cheryl Almeida & Adria Steinberg, as first appeared in *Education Week*, July 30, 2008. Reprinted with permission from Editorial Projects in Education.

CHAPTER 6
"Consensus on Learning Time Builds," by Catherine Gewertz, as first appeared in *Education Week*, September 24, 2008. Reprinted with permission from Editorial Projects in Education.
"Expanding Learning Time," by Debra Viadero, as first appeared in *Education Week*, September 30, 2008. Reprinted with permission from Editorial Projects in Education.
"High-Quality After-School Programs Tied to Test-Score Gains," by Debra Viadero, as first appeared in *Education Week*, November 28, 2008. Reprinted with permission from Editorial Projects in Education.
"Student Engagement," by Linda Jacobson, as first appeared in *Education Week*, November 5, 2008. Reprinted with permission from Editorial Projects in Education.

CHAPTER 7
"Aspiring Teachers Take Up Residence," by Vaishali Honawar, as first appeared in *Education Week*, October 14, 2008. Reprinted with permission from Editorial Projects in Education.
"Tiered Licensing Systems Being Used by States to Help Teacher Quality," by Bess Keller, as first appeared in *Education Week*, December 19, 2008. Reprinted with permission from Editorial Projects in Education.
"The Question of Performance Pay," by James W. Guthrie & Patrick J. Schuermann, as first appeared in *Education Week*, October 29, 2008. Reprinted with permission from Editorial Projects in Education.
"Seeking—and Finding—Good Teaching," by Julie Sweetland, as first appeared in *Education Week*, October 22, 2008. Reprinted with permission from Editorial Projects in Education.
"Teaching at the Precipice," by Arthur E. Levine & David Haselkorn, as first appeared in *Education Week*, November 5, 2008. Reprinted with permission from Editorial Projects in Education.
"A Marshall Plan for Teaching," by Linda Darling-Hammond, adapted from the original, which first appeared in *Education Week*, January 10, 2007. Reprinted with permission from Editorial Projects in Education.

CHAPTER 8
"Chicago District Focusing on Pathways to College," by Christina Samuels, as first appeared in *Education Week*, June 11, 2008. Reprinted with permission from Editorial Projects in Education.
"College-Cost 'Emergency' Said to Jeopardize Access," by Scott J. Cech, as first appeared in *Education Week*, December 3, 2008. Reprinted with permission from Editorial Projects in Education.
"Panel Proposes Major Overhaul of College-Aid System," by Scott J. Cech, as first appeared in *Education Week*, September 24, 2008. Reprinted with permission from Editorial Projects in Education.
"What Does 'Ready' Mean?" by Lynn Olson, as first appeared in *Education Week*, June 12, 2007. Reprinted with permission from Editorial Projects in Education.

CHAPTER 9
Advice for the President transcribed audio segments used with permission from Learning Matters, Inc.

CHAPTER 10
National Academy of Education Recommendations used with permission from the National Academy of Education.

APPENDIX
Material from the www.change.gov transition team site is republished under that site's Creative Commons Attribution 3.0 license.